# INDIA'S REBIRTH

"I write, not for the orthodox, nor for those who have discovered a new orthodoxy, Samaj or Panth, nor for the unbeliever. I write for those who acknowledge reason but do not identify reason with Western Materialism; who are sceptics but not unbelievers; who, admitting the claims of modern thought, still believe in India, her mission, her gospel, her immortal life and her eternal rebirth."

Sri Aurobindo
(c. 1911)

Out of the ruins of the West...

# INDIA'S REBIRTH

*A selection from Sri Aurobindo's
writings, talks and speeches*

INSTITUT DE RECHERCHES ÉVOLUTIVES, Paris
& MIRA ADITI, Mysore

This book was prepared by a team of researchers under the direction of Sujata Nahar. Any profits arising from its sale will be entirely devoted to the spread of Sri Aurobindo's vision of India and her future evolution.

The publisher of this book, the Institut de Recherches Évolutives ("Institute for Evolutionary Research"), has published in France the 13 volumes of *L'Agenda de Mère (Mother's Agenda)* and looks after the worldwide diffusion of Sri Aurobindo's and Mother's evolutionary experience. The co-publisher, Mira Aditi, looks after the same work in India and Asia.

This selection was prepared from Sri Aurobindo's works published by Sri Aurobindo Ashram, Pondicherry, India.


Information addresses:

— *for Asia:*

MIRA ADITI CENTRE
62 'Sriranga', 2nd Main, 1st Cross
T. K. Layout, Saraswatipuram
Mysore 570 009, India

— *for America:*

INSTITUT DE RECHERCHES ÉVOLUTIVES, CANADA
CP 41 CHAMBLY
QC
J3L 4B1 CANADA

— *for Europe:*

INSTITUT DE RECHERCHES ÉVOLUTIVES
142, boulevard du Montparnasse
75014 Paris, France


Printed at Thomson Press, Faridabad, India
ISBN 2-902776-47-0 & 81-85137-27-7
First edition, August 1993
SECOND EDITION, revised and enlarged, January 1997

To India,
the ancient Mother

to Sri Aurobindo,
who saw her reborn

## Editors' Note

*This book presents Sri Aurobindo's vision of India as it grew from his return from England in 1893, more than a hundred years ago, to his political days in the first decade of the century and finally to his forty-year-long withdrawal from public view during which he plunged into his "real work" of evolutionary action.*

*This brief chronological selection from all that Sri Aurobindo said or wrote on India, her soul and her destiny, is by no means integral, but we trust it offers a sufficiently wide view of the lines of development Sri Aurobindo wished India to follow if she was to overcome the deep-rooted obstacles standing in the way of her rebirth.*

*A few notes have been added to help put the excerpts into historical perspective, and a Chronology, list of references and Index have been provided at the end of the book.*

*This second edition has been revised and enlarged.*

# CONTENTS

*Editors' Note*  . . . . . . . . . . . . . . . . . . . . . . . . . .   5

   I.  1893 — 1910: Revolutionary Writings  . . . .   7

  II.  1910 — 1922: Essays, Letters & Articles  . . .   83

 III.  1923 — 1926: Talks (1st series)  . . . . . . . . .  163

 IV.  1929 — 1938: Letters  . . . . . . . . . . . . . . . .  187

  V.  1938 — 1940: Talks (2nd series)  . . . . . . . . .  211

 VI.  1940 — 1950: Letters & Messages  . . . . . . .  233

*Chronology*  . . . . . . . . . . . . . . . . . . . . . . . . . . .  256

*References*  . . . . . . . . . . . . . . . . . . . . . . . . . . .  260

*Index*  . . . . . . . . . . . . . . . . . . . . . . . . . . . . . .  263

# I

## 1893 — 1910

*(After thirteen years in England where he received a thoroughly Western education, Sri Aurobindo returned to India on February 6, 1893, at the age of twenty.*

*Bankim Chatterji's* Anandamath, *which contained "Bande Mataram," the hymn to the Motherland, had been published eleven years earlier. Swami Vivekananda had just come to the end of his first pilgrimage round India, and was preparing to sail for America. But it was going to take another dozen years for their call to their countrymen to find expression in the political field. For the present, the eight-year-old Indian National Congress, whose members were mostly drawn from the Anglicized upper classes of society, had full faith in British fair-mindedness and the "providential character" of British rule in India, and year after year swore its "unswerving allegiance to the British crown"; it was content with submitting petitions which were simply ignored by the Colonial rulers. There was another twelve years to go before the start of the open struggle for freedom in 1905, and twenty-five years before Mahatma Gandhi's entry on the political scene in 1918.*

*Sri Aurobindo was twenty-one when he wrote a series of nine articles, "New Lamps for Old," in the* Indu Prakash, *a Marathi-English Bombay daily; in these articles, which had to be stopped following pressures on the newspaper's editor, Sri Aurobindo took stock of the prevailing situation and launched into a detailed and forceful criticism of the "mendicant policy" of the Congress. A few extracts:)*

**August 7, 1893**

We cannot afford to raise any institution to the rank of a fetish. To do so would be simply to become the slaves of our own machinery.

*\* \* \**

9

**August 21, 1893**

Our actual enemy is not any force exterior to ourselves, but our own crying weaknesses, our cowardice, our selfishness, our hypocrisy, our purblind sentimentalism.

* *<br>*

**August 28, 1893**

I say, of the Congress, then, this—that its aims are mistaken, that the spirit in which it proceeds towards their accomplishment is not a spirit of sincerity and whole-heartedness, and that the methods it has chosen are not the right methods, and the leaders in whom it trusts, not the right sort of men to be leaders;—in brief, that we are at present the blind led, if not by the blind, at any rate by the one-eyed.

* *<br>*

**December 4, 1893**

To play with baubles is our ambition, not to deal with grave questions in a spirit of serious energy. But while we are playing with baubles, with our Legislative Councils, our Simultaneous Examinations,* our ingenious schemes for separating the judicial from the executive functions,—while we, I say, are finessing about trifles, the waters of the great deep are being stirred and that surging chaos of the primitive man over which our civilised societies are superimposed on a thin crust of convention, is being strangely and ominously agitated.

* *<br>*

---

* References to two largely meaningless reforms that the Congress was at the time begging from the British rulers.

*(On his return to India, Sri Aurobindo joined the
Baroda State Service; from 1897 to early 1906 he
taught French and English at the Baroda College,
eventually becoming its principal. These years gave
him a first-hand experience of the dismal condition of
education in India and made him feel an acute need
for a true national education.)*

### Early 1900s (?)

If the physical training it [the Indian University system]
provides is contemptible and the moral training nil, the
mental training is also meagre in quantity and worthless in
quality.... In order for a student to get a degree let us make
it absolutely necessary that he shall have a good education.
If a worthless education is sufficient in order to secure this
object and a good education quite unessential, it is obvious
that the student will not incur great trouble and diversion of
energy in order to acquire what he feels to be unnecessary.
But change this state of things, make culture and true science
essential and the same interested motive which now makes
him content with a bad education will then compel him to
strive after culture and true science.... We in India have
become so barbarous that we send our children to school
with the grossest utilitarian motive unmixed with any disin-
terested desire for knowledge; but the education we receive
is itself responsible for this....

It is a fundamental and deplorable error by which we in
this country have confused education with the acquisition of
knowledge.... Amount of knowledge is in itself not of first
importance, but to make the best use of what we know. The
easy assumption of our educationists that we have only to
supply the mind with a smattering of facts in each department of knowledge and the mind can be trusted to develop
itself and take its own suitable road is contrary to science,

contrary to human experience.... Much as we have lost as a nation, we have always preserved our intellectual alertness, quickness and originality; but even this last gift is threatened by our University system, and if it goes, it will be the beginning of irretrievable degradation and final extinction.

The very first step in reform must therefore be to revolutionise the whole aim and method of our education.[1]*

\*

Indian scholarship ... must clearly have one advantage [over the European], an intimate feeling of the language, a sensitiveness ... which the European cannot hope to possess unless he sacrifices his sense of racial superiority.... For to the European Sanskrit words are no more than dead counters which he can play with and throw as he likes into places the most unnatural or combinations the most monstrous; to the Hindu they are living things the very soul of whose temperament he understands and whose possibilities he can judge to a hair. That with these advantages Indian scholars have not been able to form themselves into a great and independent school of learning is due to two causes, the miserable scantiness of the mastery in Sanskrit provided by our universities, crippling to all but born scholars, and their lack of a sturdy independence which makes us over-ready to defer to European authority.[2]

\*
\* \*

---

* See references at the end of the book.

*(From 1900 onward, Sri Aurobindo began contacting revolutionary groups in Maharashtra and Bengal, and tried to coordinate their action with the help of his brother, Barindra Kumar Ghose, and Jatindranath Banerjee; at Sri Aurobindo's initiative, P. Mitter, Surendranath Tagore, Chittaranjan Das and Sister Nivedita soon formed the first secret council for revolutionary activities in Bengal. Although an effective coordination between the various groups remained elusive, some of them, such as P. Mitter's Anusilan Samiti, played a considerable part in spreading the Nationalist ideal. Their chief weapon was the establishment of centres in numerous towns and villages, where young men were given intellectual, moral and physical training, and were inspired to work for India's liberation.*

*Around this time, Sri Aurobindo wrote* **Bhawani Mandir,** *a pamphlet "for the revolutionary preparation of the country." Thousands of copies of it were distributed clandestinely. A few excerpts:)*

## 1905

India, the ancient Mother, is indeed striving to be reborn, striving with agony and tears, but she strives in vain. What ails her, she who is after all so vast and might be so strong? There is surely some enormous defect, something vital is wanting in us, nor is it difficult to lay our finger on the spot. We have all things else, but we are empty of strength, void of energy. We have abandoned Shakti and are therefore abandoned by Shakti. The Mother is not in our hearts, in our brains, in our arms.

The wish to be reborn we have in abundance, there is no deficiency there. How many attempts have been made, how many movements have been begun, in religion, in society, in politics! But the same fate has overtaken or is preparing to overtake them all. They flourish for a moment, then the impulse wanes, the fire dies out, and if they endure, it is only as empty shells, forms from which the Brahma has gone or in which it lies overpowered with Tamas and inert. Our beginnings are mighty, but they have neither sequel nor fruit.

Now we are beginning in another direction; we have started a great industrial movement which is to enrich and regenerate an impoverished land. Untaught by experience, we do not perceive that this movement must go the way of all the others, unless we first seek the one essential thing, unless we acquire strength.

Is it knowledge that is wanting? We Indians, born and bred in a country where Jñāna has been stored and accumulated since the race began, bear about in us the inherited gains of many thousands of years.... But it is a dead knowledge, a burden under which we are bowed, a poison which is corroding us, rather than as it should be a staff to support our feet and a weapon in our hands; for this is the nature of all great things that when they are not used or are ill used, they turn upon the bearer and destroy him....

Is it love, enthusiasm, Bhakti that is wanting? These are ingrained in the Indian nature, but in the absence of Shakti we cannot concentrate, we cannot direct, we cannot even preserve it. Bhakti is the leaping flame, Shakti is the fuel. If the fuel is scanty how long can the fire endure?...

The deeper we look, the more we shall be convinced that the one thing wanting, which we must strive to acquire before all others, is strength—strength physical, strength mental, strength moral, but above all strength spiritual which is the one inexhaustible and imperishable source of all the others. If we have strength everything else will be added to us easily and naturally. In the absence of strength we are like men in a dream who have hands but cannot seize or strike, who have feet but cannot run....

If India is to survive, she must be made young again. Rushing and billowing streams of energy must be poured into her; her soul must become, as it was in the old times, like the surges, vast, puissant, calm or turbulent at will, an ocean of action or of force.

Many of us, utterly overcome by Tamas, the dark and heavy demon of inertia, are saying nowadays that it is impossible, that India is decayed, bloodless and lifeless, too weak ever to recover; that our race is doomed to extinction. It is a foolish and idle saying. No man or nation need be weak unless he chooses, no man or nation need perish unless he deliberately chooses extinction.

For what is a nation? What is our mother-country? It is not a piece of earth, nor a figure of speech, nor a fiction of the mind. It is a mighty Shakti, composed of the Shaktis of all the millions of units that make up the nation, just as Bhawani Mahisha Mardini sprang into being from the Shakti of all the millions of gods assembled in one mass of force and welded into unity. The Shakti we call India, Bhawani Bharati, is the living unity of the Shaktis of three hundred million people,* but she is inactive, imprisoned in the magic circle of Tamas, the self-indulgent inertia and ignorance of her sons....

We have to create strength where it did not exist before; we have to change our natures, and become new men with new hearts, to be born again.... We need a nucleus of men in whom the Shakti is developed to its uttermost extent, in whom it fills every corner of the personality and overflows to fertilise the earth. These, having the fire of Bhawani in their hearts and brains, will go forth and carry the flame to every nook and cranny of our land.

*<br>* *

---

* The population of India, which at the time included present-day Pakistan and Bangladesh.

*(From a letter Sri Aurobindo wrote in Bengali to his wife, Mrinalini Devi, in which he tried to explain to her the call he felt to work for his country's freedom; this letter was seized by the police a few years later and produced as evidence in the Alipore Bomb Case.)*

**August 30, 1905**

While others look upon their country as an inert piece of matter—a few meadows and fields, forests and hills and rivers—I look upon my country as the Mother. I adore Her, I worship Her as the Mother. What would a son do if a demon sat on his mother's breast and started sucking her blood?... I know I have the strength to deliver this fallen race. It is not physical strength—I am not going to fight with sword or gun —but the strength of knowledge....[3]

*<br>* *

*(Alarmed by the rising force of Bengali feeling against British rule, Lord Curzon, the Viceroy, partitioned Bengal in 1905. This faithful application of the "divide-and-rule" policy aimed both at breaking the growing political agitation in Bengal and at using the Muslim-dominated East Bengal as the thin end of a wedge between Hindus and Muslims—a policy that was to culminate in the partition of India forty years later.*

*Bengal responded to its partition by massive and unanimous protests, in which many personalities took part, such as Rabindranath Tagore, Surendranath Banerji, Bepin Chandra Pal, Ashwini Kumar Dutt.... The ideal of Swadeshi, which called for the boycott of British goods, spread widely.*

*In March, 1906, Barin Ghose with a few others started the fiery Bengali weekly, the* Yugantar, *to which Sri Aurobindo contributed several articles. In August, B. C. Pal launched the famous English daily, the* Bande Mataram; *Sri Aurobindo joined it and soon took up its editorship, side by side with his behind-the-scenes activities with, among others, Bal Gangadhar Tilak and Lala Lajpat Rai.*

*Day after day till May, 1908, Sri Aurobindo used the pages of the* Bande Mataram *to breathe inspiration, force and clarity of purpose into the nascent Nationalist movement; his first preoccupation, in the face of fierce opposition from the British authorities, the self-righteous Anglo-Indian press and most of the Congress Moderates, was in his own words "to declare openly for complete and absolute independence as the aim of political action in India and to insist on this persistently in the pages of the journal; [Sri Aurobindo] was the first politician in India who had the courage to do this in public and he was immediately successful. The [Nationalist] party took up the word Swaraj to express its own ideal of independence and it soon spread everywhere.... The greatest thing done in those years was the creation of a new spirit in the country."[4] The following passages are from the* Bande Mataram.*)*

**September 1, 1906**

The true policy of the Congress movement should have been from the beginning to gather together under its flag all the elements of strength that exist in this huge country. The Brahman Pandit and the Mahomedan Maulavi, the caste organisation and the trade-union, the labourer and the artisan, the coolie at his work and the peasant in his field, none of these should have been left out of the sphere of our activities. For each is a strength, a unit of force; and in politics the victory is to the side which can marshal the largest and most closely serried number of such units and handle them most skilfully, not to those who can bring forward the best arguments or talk the most eloquently.

But the Congress started from the beginning with a misconception of the most elementary facts of politics and with its eyes turned towards the British Government and away from the people.

*
* *

**September 4, 1906**

We objected so strongly to this measure [Bengal's Partition] because it was calculated to strike a serious blow at the political power of the Bengalee-speaking race. Our second objection was that it was professedly wanted by the Government to create a Mahomedan province with Dacca as its capital, and the evident object of it was to sow discord between the Hindus and the Mahomedans in a Province that had never known it in the whole history of the present British connection.... There is in [the present] agitation a consciousness of a new strength, the quickening of a new life, the inspiration of a new ideal. This agitation is not an agitation merely against Partition or against any other particular measure of the Government.... The attainment of absolute national autonomy,—it is this alone that will settle down this movement....*

The idea that by encouraging Mahomedan rowdyism, the present agitation may be put down, is preposterous; and those who cherish this notion forget that the bully is neither the strongest nor the bravest of men; and [they think] that because the self-restraint of the Hindu, miscalled cowardice, has been a prominent feature of his national character, he is absolutely incapable of striking straight and striking hard when any sacred situation demands this. Nor has it been proved even in recent British-concocted disputes between Hindus and Mahomedans in different parts of India, that the mild Hindu is so absolutely helpless and incapable of defending his rights and liberties as he is painted to be by his foreign enemies.

\* \*
\*

**September 13, 1906**

The idea that the election of a Mahomedan President will conciliate the anti-Congress Mahomedans is a futility which has been repeatedly exposed by experience.

\*

Ever since the birth of the Congress, those who have been in the leadership of this great National Movement have persistently denied the general public in the country the right of determining what shall and what shall not be said or done on their behalf and in their name. The delegates have been gathered from all parts of the country, not to deliberate upon public matters, but simply to lend their support to the decisions that had already been arrived at by secret conclaves of half a dozen men.

---

* This is one of the first times, if not the first, that an Indian had the courage to publicly call for India's complete independence.

**December 31, 1906**

The leaders can only deserve reverence by acting in the spirit of the chief servants of their country and not in the spirit of masters and dictators.

*
* *

**April 5, 1907**

Politics is the work of the Kshatriya and it is the virtues of the Kshatriya we must develop if we are to be morally fit for freedom.

*
* *

**April 8, 1907**

We reiterate with all the emphasis we can command that the Kshatriya of old must again take his rightful position in our social polity to discharge the first and foremost duty of defending its interests. The brain is impotent without the right arm of strength.

*
* *

**April 13, 1907**

We should be absolutely unsparing in our attack on whatever obstructs the growth of the nation, and never be afraid to call a spade a spade. Excessive good nature, *chakshu lajjā* [the desire to be always pleasant and polite], will never do in serious politics. Respect of persons must always give place to truth and conscience; and the demand that we should be silent because of the age or past services of our opponents, is politically immoral and unsound. Open attack, unsparing criticism, the severest satire, the most wounding irony, are all methods perfectly justifiable and indispensable in politics.

We have strong things to say; let us say them strongly; we have stern things to do; let us do them sternly. But there is always a danger of strength degenerating into violence and sternness into ferocity, and that should be avoided so far as it is humanly possible.

*
* *

## April 16, 1907

There are periods in the history of the world when the unseen Power that guides its destinies seems to be filled with a consuming passion for change and a strong impatience of the old. The Great Mother, the Adya Shakti, has resolved to take the nations into Her hand and shape them anew. These are periods of rapid destruction and energetic creation, filled with the sound of cannon and the trampling of armies, the crash of great downfalls, and the turmoil of swift and violent revolutions; the world is thrown into the smelting pot and comes out in a new shape and with new features. They are periods when the wisdom of the wise is confounded and the prudence of the prudent turned into a laughing-stock....

*

The supreme service of Bankim [Chandra Chatterji] to his nation was that he gave us the vision of our Mother.... It is not till the Motherland reveals herself to the eye of the mind as something more than a stretch of earth or a mass of individuals, it is not till she takes shape as a great Divine and Maternal Power in a form of beauty that can dominate the mind and seize the heart that ... the patriotism that works miracles and saves a doomed nation is born....

It was thirty-two years ago that Bankim wrote his great song and few listened; but in a sudden moment of awakening from long delusions the people of Bengal looked round for the truth and in a fated moment somebody sang *Bande Mataram*. The Mantra had been given and in a single day a whole people had been converted to the religion of patriotism. The Mother had revealed herself.

*
* *

**April 23, 1907**

Each nation must practise the political creed which is the most suited to its temperament and circumstances; for that is the best for it which leads most surely and completely to national liberty and national self-realisation.

*
* *

**May 11, 1907**

In this grave crisis of our destinies let not our people lose their fortitude or suffer stupefaction and depression to seize upon and unnerve their souls. The fight in which we are engaged is not like the wars of old in which when the king or leader fell, the army fled. The King whom we follow to the wars today, is our own Motherland, the sacred and imperishable; the leader of our onward march is the Almighty Himself, that element within and without us whom sword cannot slay, nor water drown, nor fire burn, nor exile divide from us, nor a prison confine.
. . .
Let there be no fainting of heart and no depression, and also let there be no unforeseeing fury, no blindly-striking madness. We are at the beginning of a time of terrible trial. The passage is not to be easy, the crown is not to be cheaply earned. India is going down into the valley of the shadow of death, into a great horror of darkness and suffering. Let us realise that what we are now suffering, is a small part of

what we shall have to suffer, and work in that knowledge, with resolution, without hysteria.... The first need at the present moment is courage, a courage which knows not how to flinch or shrink.

\* \*
\*

**May 23, 1907**

Where the will of a higher Power is active in a great upheaval, no individual is indispensable.

\* \*
\*

**May 28, 1907**

We have to fill the minds of our boys from childhood with the idea of the country, and present them with that idea at every turn and make their whole young life a lesson in the practice of the virtues which afterwards go to make the patriot and the citizen. If we do not attempt this, we may as well give up our desire to create an Indian nation altogether; for without such a discipline nationalism, patriotism, regeneration are mere words and ideas which can never become a part of the very soul of the nation and never therefore a great realised fact. Mere academical teaching of patriotism is of no avail.

\* \*
\*

**June 7, 1907**

What India needs especially at this moment is the aggressive virtues, the spirit of soaring idealism, bold creation, fearless resistance, courageous attack; of the passive tamasic spirit of inertia we have already too much. We need to cultivate another training and temperament, another habit of mind. We would apply to the present situation the vigourous motto of Danton, that what we need, what we should learn above all things is to dare and again to dare and still to dare.

*
* *

**June 19, 1907**

Apart from the natural attachment which every man has to his country, its literature, its traditions, its customs and usages, patriotism has an additional stimulus in the acknowledged excellence of a national civilisation. If Britons love England with all her faults, why should we fail to love India whose faults were whittled down to an irreducible minimum till foreign conquests threw the whole society out of gear? But instead of being dominated by the natural ambition of carrying the banner of such a civilisation all over the world, we are unable to maintain its integrity in its own native home. This is betraying a trust. This is unworthiness of the worst type. We have not been able to add anything to this precious bequest; on the contrary we have been keeping ourselves and generations yet unborn from a full enjoyment of their lawful heritage....

According to Sidgwick,* physical expansion proceeds from a desire for spiritual expansion and history also supports the assertion. But why should not India then be the first power in the world? Who else has the undisputed right to extend spiritual sway over the world? This was Swami Vivekananda's plan of campaign. India can once more be made conscious of her greatness by an overmastering sense of the greatness of her spirituality. This sense of greatness is the main feeder of

---

* A writer who, defending British imperialism, spoke of "the justifiable pride which the cultivated members of a civilised community feel in the beneficent exercise of dominion and in the performance by their nation of the noble task of spreading the highest kind of civilisation [*sic*!]."

all patriotism. This only can put an end to all self-depreciation and generate a burning desire to recover the lost ground.

*   *   *

**June 22, 1907**

He [a leader in Bengal] has not the qualities of a politician —robustness, backbone, the ability to will a certain course of action and the courage to carry it out.... No man who shrinks from struggle or is appalled by the thought of aggression can hope to seize and lead the wild forces that are rising to the surface in twentieth-century India.

*   *   *

**July 3, 1907**

The East is more ancient by many thousands of years than the West, but a greater length of years does not necessarily imply a more advanced age.... Asia is long-lived, Europe brief, ephemeral. Asia is in everything hugely mapped, immense and grandiose in its motions, and its life-periods are measured accordingly. Europe lives by centuries, Asia by millenniums. Europe is parcelled out in nations, Asia in civilisations. The whole of Europe forms only one civilisation with a common, derived and largely second-hand culture; Asia supports three civilisations, each of them original and of the soil. Everything in Europe is small, rapid and short-lived; she has not the secret of immortality.

*   *   *

**July 25, 1907**

Spiritual power in the present creates material power in the future and for this reason we always find that if it is material force which dominates the present, it is spiritual which moulds and takes possession of the future....

Since the spiritual life of India is the first necessity of the world's future, we fight not only for our own political and spiritual freedom but for the spiritual emancipation of the human race.... For it is not among an enslaved, degraded and perishing people that the Rishis and great spirits can continue to be born.

*
* *

*(On August 15, 1906, a few days after the start of the* Bande Mataram, *the Bengal National College had opened in Calcutta with Sri Aurobindo as its Principal; it was one of the first experiments in the search for a true national education. Its foundation had been made possible by the generous financial assistance of Subodh Mullick, one of Sri Aurobindo's collaborators in his secret action. In spite of his charge of the* Bande Mataram, *Sri Aurobindo found time to teach Indian history and geography, English history, political science, as well as French, German and English....*

*A year later, on August 16, 1907, the British government, alarmed by the spread and impact of the* Bande Mataram, *arrested Sri Aurobindo under a sedition law; he had turned thirty-five the day before. He owed his acquittal a month later to the government's failure to prove that he was the editor of the dreaded journal. It was then that Rabindranath Tagore wrote his famous poem to Sri Aurobindo, whom he saluted as "the voice incarnate, free, of India's soul."*

*A few days after his arrest, Sri Aurobindo, released on bail, resigned his post of Principal of the Bengal National College. A few excerpts from a speech he delivered before the students and teachers, who had assembled to express their "heart-felt sympathy.")*

## August 23, 1907

When we established this college and left other occupations, other chances of life, to devote our lives to this institution, we did so because we hoped to see in it the foundation, the nucleus of a nation, of the new India which is to begin its career after this night of sorrow and trouble, on that day of glory and greatness when India will work for the world. What we want here is not merely to give you a little information, not merely to open to you careers for earning a livelihood, but to build up sons for the Motherland to work and to suffer for her. That is why we started this college and that is the work to which I want you to devote yourselves in future. What has been insufficiently and imperfectly begun by us, it is for you to complete and lead to perfection. When I come back I wish to see some of you becoming rich, rich not for yourselves but that you may enrich the Mother with your riches. I wish to see some of you becoming great, great not for your own sakes, not that you may satisfy your own vanity, but great for her, to make India great, to enable her to stand up with head erect among the nations of the earth, as she did in days of yore when the world looked up to her for light. Even those who will remain poor and obscure, I want to see their very poverty and obscurity devoted to the Motherland. There are times in a nation's history when Providence places before it one work, one aim, to which everything else, however high and noble in itself, has to be sacrificed. Such a time has now arrived for our Motherland when nothing is dearer than her service, when everything else is to be directed to that end.... Work that she may prosper. Suffer that she may rejoice. All is contained in that one single advice.

*<br>* *

### September 22, 1907

Caste was originally an arrangement for the distribution of functions in society, just as much as class in Europe, but the principle on which the distribution was based in India was peculiar to this country.... A Brahmin was a Brahmin not by mere birth, but because he discharged the duty of preserving the spiritual and intellectual elevation of the race, and he had to cultivate the spiritual temperament and acquire the spiritual training which could alone qualify him for the task.

The Kshatriya was a Kshatriya not merely because he was the son of warriors and princes, but because he discharged the duty of protecting the country and preserving the high courage and manhood of the nation, and he had to cultivate the princely temperament and acquire the strong and lofty Samurai training which alone fitted him for his duties. So it was with the Vaishya whose function was to amass wealth for the race and the Sudra who discharged the humbler duties of service without which the other castes could not perform their share of labour for the common good.... Essentially there was, between the devout Brahmin and the devout Sudra, no inequality in the single *virāt purusa* [Cosmic Spirit] of which each was a necessary part. Chokha Mela, the Maratha Pariah, became the Guru of Brahmins proud of their caste purity; the Chandala taught Shankaracharya: for the Brahman was revealed in the body of the Pariah and in the Chandala there was the utter presence of Shiva the Almighty....

Caste therefore was not only an institution which ought to be immune from the cheap second-hand denunciations so long in fashion, but a supreme necessity without which Hindu civilisation could not have developed its distinctive character or worked out its unique mission.

But to recognise this is not to debar ourselves from pointing out its later perversions and desiring its transformation. It is the nature of human institutions to degenerate, to lose their vitality, and decay, and the first sign of decay is the loss of flexibility and oblivion of the essential spirit in which they were conceived. The spirit is permanent, the body changes; and a body which refuses to change must die. The spirit expresses itself in many ways while itself remaining essentially the same but the body must change to suit its changing environments if it wishes to live. There is no doubt that the institution of caste degenerated. It ceased to be determined by spiritual qualifications which, once essential, have now come to be subordinate and even immaterial and is determined by the purely material tests of occupation and birth. By this change it has set itself against the fundamental tendency of Hinduism which is to insist on the spiritual and subordinate the material and thus lost most of its meaning. The spirit of caste arrogance, exclusiveness and superiority came to dominate it instead of the spirit of duty, and the change weakened the nation and helped to reduce us to our present conditions.

\*
\* \*

**October 7, 1907**

This great and ancient nation was once the fountain of human light, the apex of human civilisation, the examplar of courage and humanity, the perfection of good Government and settled society, the mother of all religions, the teacher of all wisdom and philosophy. It has suffered much at the hands of inferior civilisations and more savage peoples; it has gone down into the shadow of night and tasted often of the bitterness of death. Its pride has been trampled into the dust and its glory has departed. Hunger and misery and despair have become the masters of this fair soil, these noble hills, these ancient rivers, these cities whose life story goes back into prehistoric night. But do you think that therefore God has utterly abandoned us and given us up for ever to be a mere convenience for the West, the helots of its commerce, and the feeders of its luxury and pride? We are still God's chosen people and all our calamities have been but a discipline of suffering, because for the great mission before us prosperity was not sufficient, adversity had also its training; to taste the glory of power and beneficence and joy was not sufficient, the knowledge of weakness and torture and humiliation was also needed; it was not enough that we should be able to fill the role of the merciful sage and the beneficent king, we had also to experience in our own persons the feelings of the outcaste and the slave.

\*
\* \*

**October 23, 1907**

There is a cant phrase which is always on our lips in season and out of season, and it is the cry for unity. We call it a cant phrase because those who use it, have not the slightest conception of what they mean when they use it, but simply employ it as an effective formula to discourage independence in thought and progressiveness in action. It is not the reality of united thought and action which they desire, it is merely the appearance of unity.... It is a habit of mind born of the spirit of dependence and weakness. It is a fosterer of falsehood and encourages cowardice and insincerity. "Be your views what they may, suppress them, for they will spoil our unity; swallow your principles, they will spoil our unity; do not battle for what you think to be the right, it will spoil our unity; leave necessary things undone, for the attempt to do them will spoil our unity;" this is the cry. The prevalence of a dead and lifeless unity is the true index of national degradation, quite as much as the prevalence of a living unity is the index of national greatness.

\* \*
\*

**December 6, 1907**

[The British] began of course long ago, the attempt to make capital of the religious diversities of Indian society and recently the policy of setting the Mahomedans as a counterpoise to the Hindus has been openly adopted.\* In the new Legislative Councils the Mahomedans are to have representation not as children of the soil, an integral portion of one Indian people, but as a politically distinct and hostile interest which will, it is hoped, outweigh or at least nullify the Hindus.... The Hindus have become self-conscious, they have heard a voice that cries

---

\* This policy led two years later to the Morley-Minto reforms (see pp. 62 & 64). The first meeting of the Muslim League was held at Karachi on December 29, 1907.

to them, "Arise from the dead, live and follow me," and they are irresistibly growing into a living and powerful political force.
...
The latest brilliant device [of the British bureaucracy] is an attempt to reshuffle the constituent elements of Indian politics and sort them out afresh on the basis not only of creed, but of caste.... [Caste] has not and should not be allowed to have any political meaning.

*<br>* *

**December 17, 1907**

When the word of the Eternal has gone abroad, when the spirit moves over the waters and the waters stir and life begins to form, then it is a law that all energies are forced to direct themselves, consciously or unconsciously, willingly or against their will, to the one supreme work of the time, the formation of the new manifest and organised life which is in process of creation....

Nationalism* depends for its success on the awakening and organising of the whole strength of the nation; it is therefore vitally important for Nationalism that the politically backward classes should be awakened and brought into the current of political life; the great mass of orthodox Hinduism which was hardly even touched by the old Congress movement, the great slumbering mass of Islam which has remained politically inert throughout the last century, the shopkeepers, the artisan class, the immense body of illiterate and ignorant peasantry, the submerged classes, even the wild tribes and races still outside the pale of Hindu civilisation, Nationalism can afford to neglect and omit none....

What Nationalism asks is for life first and above all things;

---

* Sri Aurobindo seldom used the words "Extremism" or "Extremist Party," which were the British government's and the Congress Moderates' derogatory designation of the Nationalist movement.

life, and still more life, is its cry. Let us by every means get rid of the pall of death which stifled us, let us dispel first the passivity, quiescence, the unspeakable oppression of inertia which has so long been our curse; that is the first and imperative need.

*
* *

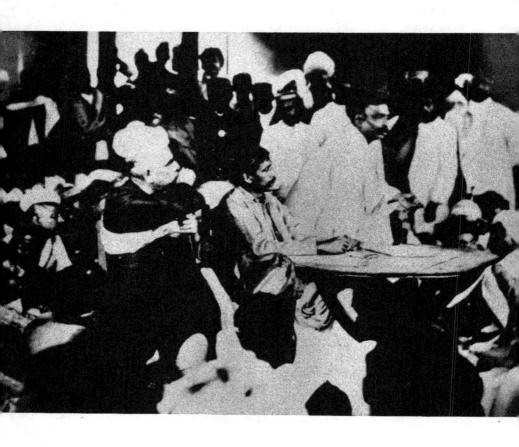

*Sri Aurobindo presiding over the Nationalists'
conference at Surat. On his right is G. S. Khaparde;
on his left, standing, is B. G. Tilak.*

*(On December 27, 1907, the Nationalist party, with Sri Aurobindo presiding over its conference, broke away from the Congress Moderates at the tumultuous Surat session over the latter's refusal to reaffirm the demands of Swaraj, Swadeshi, Boycott and National Education, which had been adopted at the previous Calcutta session under the presidentship of Dadabhai Naoroji. It was going to take the Congress another twenty-two years to declare complete independence for its goal.)*

**January 19, 1908**

*(A few days after the Surat events, Sri Aurobindo had in Baroda a first decisive experience, that of Nirvana or the Brahman consciousness. Henceforth all his activities, including his speeches and writings, flowed from an "absolute silence of the mind."*
*On his way back to Calcutta, Sri Aurobindo was asked to speak at many places. A few excerpts from a speech he gave before a large gathering at the Mahajan Wadi in Bombay:)*

Belief is not a merely intellectual process, belief is not a mere persuasion of the mind, belief is something that is in our heart, and what you believe, you must do, because belief is from God. It is to the heart that God speaks, it is in the heart that God resides.... Here is a work that you have undertaken, a work so gigantic, so stupendous, the means for which are so poor, the resistance to which will be so strong, so organised ... and what means have you with which to carry out this tremendous work of yours? If you look at it intellectually, it is hopeless.... This intellectual process, if it is used honestly, if it is followed to the very end, leads you to despair. It leads you to death.

. . .

What is the one thing needful? What is it that has helped the older men [of the Nationalist movement] who have gone to prison?... They have had one and all of them consciously or unconsciously one over-mastering idea, one idea which nothing can shake, and this was the idea that there is a great Power at work to help India, and that we are doing what it bids us.... They have this conviction within, not in the intellect but in the heart, that the Power that is guiding them is invincible, that it is Almighty, that it is immortal and irresistible and that it will do its work. They have nothing to do. They have simply to obey that Power. They have simply to go where it leads them. They have only to speak the words that it tells them to speak, and to do the thing that it tells them to do.... He himself is behind us. He himself is the worker and the work. He is immortal in the hearts of his people....

When you believe in God, when you believe that God is guiding you, believe that God is doing all and that you are doing nothing,—what is there to fear?... There is nothing to fear.... What can all these tribunals, what can all the powers of the world do to That which is within you, that Immortal, that Unborn and Undying One, whom the sword cannot pierce, whom the fire cannot burn, and whom the water cannot drown? Him the jail cannot confine and the gallows cannot end. What is there that you can fear when you are conscious of Him who is within you? Courage is then a necessity, courage is natural and courage is inevitable.... You are protected through life and death by One who survives in the very hour of death, you feel your immortality in the hour of your worst sufferings, you feel you are invincible....

Try to realise the strength within you, try to bring it forward, so that everything you do may be not your own doing, but the doing of that Truth within you. Try so that every hour that you live shall be enlightened by that presence, that every thought of yours shall be inspired from that one fountain of inspiration, that every faculty and quality in you may be

placed at the service of that immortal Power within you....
The leader is within yourselves.

* * *

**February 19, 1908**

When a great people rises from the dust, what *mantra* is
the *sanjīvanī mantra*\* or what power is the resurrecting
force of its resurgence? In India there are two great *mantras*,
the *mantra* of "Bande Mataram" which is the public and
universal cry of awakened love of Motherland, and there is
another more secret and mystic which is not yet revealed.

* * *

**February 20, 1908**

Truth is the rock on which the world is built. *Satyena
tisthate jagat.* Falsehood can never be the true source of
strength. When falsehood is at the root of a movement, that
movement is doomed to failure. Diplomacy can only help a
movement if the movement proceeds upon truth. To make
diplomacy the root-principle is to contravene the laws of
existence.

* * *

**February 22, 1908**

Whatever plans we may make, we shall find quite useless
when the time for action comes. Revolutions are always full
of surprises, and whoever thinks he can play chess with a
revolution will soon find how terrible is the grasp of God and
how insignificant the human reason before the whirlwind of

---

\* A mantra capable of bringing a dead man back to life.

His breath. That man only is likely to dominate the chances of a Revolution, who makes no plans but preserves his heart pure for the will of God to declare itself. The great rule of life is to have no schemes but one unalterable purpose. If the will is fixed on the purpose it sets itself to accomplish, then circumstances will suggest the right course; but the schemer finds himself always tripped up by the unexpected.

*
* *

**February 24, 1908**

National education cannot be defined briefly in one or two sentences, but we may describe it tentatively as the education which starting with the past and making full use of the present builds up a great nation. Whoever wishes to cut off the nation from its past is no friend of our national growth. Whoever fails to take advantage of the present is losing us the battle of life. We must therefore save for India all that she has stored up of knowledge, character and noble thought in her immemorial past. We must acquire for her the best knowledge that Europe can give her and assimilate it to her own peculiar type of national temperament. We must introduce the best methods of teaching humanity has developed, whether modern or ancient. And all these we must harmonise into a system which will be impregnated with the spirit of self-reliance so as to build up men and not machines....

*
* *

**March 5, 1908**

India is the *guru* of the nations, the physician of the human soul in its profounder maladies; she is destined once more to new-mould the life of the world....

*
* *

**March 6, 1908**

When the poison of Western education was first poured into our veins, it had its immediate effect, and the Hindus [of Bengal], who were then the majority of the Bengali-speaking population, began to stream away from the village to the town....

Only the race which does not sacrifice the soundness of its rural root of life to the urban brilliance of its foliage and flowering, is in a sound condition and certain of permanence.... We must now turn to the one field of work in this direction which we have most neglected, the field of agriculture. The return to the land is as essential to our salvation as the development of Swadeshi or the fight against famine. If we train our young men to go back to the fields, they will be able to become mentors, leaders and examples to the village population.... The problem is urgent in its call for a solution, and the mere organisation of village associations will be only partially effective if it is not backed up by a system of instruction which will bring the educated Hindu back to the soil as a farmer himself and a local leader of the peasantry of the race.

*
* *

**March 16, 1908**

It has been said that democracy is based on the rights of man; it has been replied that it should rather take its stand on the duties of man; but both rights and duties are European ideas. Dharma is the Indian conception in which rights and duties lose the artificial antagonism created by a view of the world which makes selfishness the root of action, and regain their deep and eternal unity. Dharma is the basis of democracy which Asia must recognise, for in this lies the distinction between the soul of Asia and the soul of Europe.

*
* *

**March 28, 1908**

We are Hindus and naturally spiritual in our temperament, because the work which we have to do for humanity is
a work which no other nation can accomplish.... The grand
workshop of spiritual experiment, the laboratory of the soul
has been India....

\*
\* \*

**March 31, 1908**

The increasing poverty of the masses has been the subject
of innumerable pamphlets, speeches and newspaper articles,
but we are apt to think our duty done when we have proved
that the poverty problem is there; we leave the solution to
the future and forget that by the time the solution comes, the
masses will have sunk into a condition of decay from which
it will take the nation many decades to recover. We have
been accustomed to deal only with the economical side of this
poverty, but there is a moral side which is even more important. The Indian peasantry have always been distinguished
from the less civilised masses of Europe by their superior
piety, gentleness, sobriety, purity, thrift and native intelligence. They are now being brutalised by unexampled oppression;\* attracted to the liquor shops which a benevolent
Government liberally supplies, bestialised by the example of
an increasingly immoral aristocracy and gradually driven to
the same habits of looseness and brutality which disgrace
the European proletariats. This degeneration is proceeding

---

\* Sri Aurobindo is referring not only to the exactions of the Zamindars, but
also to the British planters' cruel treatment of the peasantry and the
ruthless imposition of high taxes which greatly impoverished it, often
resulting in recurring famines. The huge drain of wealth to Britain from all
fields of India's economic life was well documented at the time in Dadabhai
Naoroji's *Poverty and Un-British Rule in India* (1876), in Romesh Dutt's
*Economic History of India* (1901), and in Sakharam Ganesh Deuskar's *Desher
Katha* (1904); the last two books, in particular, had a great influence on the
birth of the Swadeshi movement.

with an alarming rapidity. In some parts of the country it has gone so far that recovery seems impossible.... We have heard of villages where the liquor shop and the prostitute, institutions unknown twenty-five years ago, have now the mastery of the poorest villagers. Many of the villages in West Bengal are now well supplied with these essentials of Western civilisation.... These conditions of the worst districts tend to become general and unless something is done to stem the tide of evil, it will sweep away the soul of India in its turbid current and leave only a shapeless monstrosity of all that is worst in human nature.

*
* *

## April 11, 1908

The Mother's feet are on the threshold, but she waits to hear the true cry, the cry that rushes out from the heart, before she will enter.... The Mother asks us for no schemes, no plans, no methods. She herself will provide the schemes, the plans, the methods better than any we can devise. She asks us for our hearts, our lives, nothing less, nothing more.
...
Regeneration is literally re-birth, and re-birth comes not by the intellect, not by the fullness of the purse, not by policy, not by change of machinery, but by the getting of a new heart, by throwing away all that we were into the fire of sacrifice and being reborn in the Mother. Self-abandonment is the demand made upon us. She asks of us, "How many will live for me? How many will die for me?" and awaits our answer.

*
* *

## April 12, 1908

Do not be afraid of obstacles in your path, it does not matter how great the forces are that stand in your way.... Do not think that anything is impossible when miracles are being worked on every side. If you are true to yourself there is nothing to be afraid of. There is nothing unattainable by truth, love and faith. This is your whole gospel which will work out miracles.

*<br>* *

### April 14, 1908

Distrust is the atmosphere of modern politics, mutual suspicion and hatred the secret spring of action. Under the fair outside of its material civilisation, a deep-seated moral disease is at work eating into the vitals of European society of which a thousand symptoms strike the eye.... If India follows in the footsteps of Europe, accepts her political ideals, social system, economic principles, she will be overcome with the same maladies. Such a consummation is neither for the good of India nor for the good of Europe. If India becomes an intellectual province of Europe, she will never attain to her natural greatness or fulfil the possibilities within her. *Paradharmah bhayāvahah*, to accept the dharma of another is perilous; it deprives the man or the nation of its secret of life and vitality and substitutes an unnatural and stunted growth for the free, large and organic development of Nature. Whenever a nation has given up the purpose of its existence, it has been at the cost of its growth. India must remain India if she is to fulfil her destiny. Nor will Europe profit by grafting her civilisation on India, for if India, who is the distinct physician of Europe's maladies, herself falls into the clutches of the disease, the disease will remain uncured and uncurable and European civilisation will perish as it perished when Rome declined, first by dry rot within itself and last by irruption from without.

*<br>* *

**April (?), 1908**

We knew so little of life that we expected others who lived on our service to prepare our freedom, so little of history that we thought reform could precede liberty, so little of science that we believed an organism could be reshaped from outside. We were ruled by shopkeepers and consented enthusiastically to think of them as angels. We affected virtues we were given no opportunity of assimilating and lost those our fathers had handed down to us. All this in perfect good faith, in the full belief that we were Europeanising ourselves and moving rapidly toward political, social, economical, moral, intellectual progress. The consummation of our political progress was a Congress which yearly passed resolutions it had no power to put in practice, statesmen whose highest function was to ask questions which need not even be answered, councillors who would have been surprised if they had been consulted, politicians who did not even know that a Right never lives until it has a Might to support it. Socially we have initiated by a few petty mechanical changes a feeble attempt to revivify the very basis of our society, which [failed to] be equal to so high a task; a spiritual renovation was hardly even attempted; economically, we attained great success in destroying our industries and enslaving ourselves to the British trader; morally, we successfully compassed the disintegration of the old moral ideas and habits and substituted for them a superficial respectability; intellectually, we prided ourselves on the tricking out of our minds in a few leavings, scraps and strays of European thought at the sacrifice of an immense and eternal heritage. Never was an education more remote from all that education truly denotes....

British rule, Britain's civilising mission in India has been the record success in history in the hypnosis of a nation. It persuaded us to live in a death of the will and its activities, taking a series of hallucinations for real things and creating in ourselves the condition of morbid weakness the hypnotist desired, until the Master of a mightier hypnosis laid His finger on India's eyes and cried, "Awake." Then only the spell was broken, the slumbering mind realised itself and the dead soul lived again.*

. . .

The new [Nationalism] overleaps every barrier; it calls to the clerk at his counter, the trader in his shop, the peasant at his plough; it summons the Brahmin from his temple and takes the hand of the Chandala in his degradation; it seeks out the student in his College, the schoolboy at his book, it touches the very child in its mother's arms; and the secluded zenana has thrilled to its voice; its eye searches the jungle for the Santal and travels the hills for the wild tribes of the mountains. It cares nothing for age or sex or caste or wealth or education or respectability; it mocks at the talk of a stake in the country; it spurns aside the demand for a property qualification or a certificate of literacy. It speaks to the illiterate or the man in the street in such rude vigorous language as he best understands, to youth and the enthusiast in accents of poetry, in language of fire, to the thinker in the terms of philosophy and logic, to the Hindu it repeats the name of Kālī, the Mahomedan it spurs to action for the glory of Islam. It cries to all to come forth, to help in God's work and remake a nation, each with what his creed or his culture, his strength, his manhood or his genius can give to the new nationality. The only qualification it asks for is a body made in the womb of an Indian mother, a heart that can feel for India, a brain that can think and plan for her greatness, a tongue that can adore her name or hands that can fight in her quarrel.... [The new Nationalism] is the rebirth in India of the Kshatriya, the Samurai.[5]

*

Man is of a less terrestrial mould than some would have

---

* An allusion to the 1905 awakening.

him to be. He has an element of the divine which the practical politician ignores. The practical politician looks to the position at the moment and imagines that he has taken everything into consideration. He has indeed studied the surface and the immediate surroundings, but he has missed what lies beyond material vision. He has left out of account the divine, the incalculable in man, that element which upsets the calculations of the schemer and disconcerts the wisdom of the diplomat.[6]

\*

The Nationalist never loses sight of the truth that law was made for man and not man for the law. Its chief function and reason for existence is to safeguard and foster the growth and happy flowering into strength and health of national life and a law which does not subserve this end or which opposes and contradicts this end, however rigidly it may enforce peace, order and security, forfeits its claim to respect and obedience. Nationalism refuses to accept Law as a fetish or peace and security as an aim in themselves.... It will not prefer violent or strenuous methods simply because they are violent or strenuous, but neither will it cling to mild and peaceful methods simply because they are mild and peaceful. It asks of a method whether it is effective for its purpose, whether it is worthy of a great people struggling to be, whether it is educative of national strength and activity, and these things ascertained, it asks nothing farther.[7]

\*

A certain class of minds shrink from aggressiveness as if it were a sin. Their temperament forbids them to feel the delight of battle and they look on what they cannot understand as something monstrous and sinful. "Heal hate by love, drive out injustice by justice, slay sin by righteousness" is their cry. Love is a sacred name, but it is easier to speak of love than to love.... The Gita is the best answer to those who shrink from battle as a sin and aggression as a lowering of morality.

. . .

It is a barren philosophy which applies a mechanical rule to all actions, or takes a word and tries to fit all human life into it. The sword of the warrior is as necessary to the fulfilment of justice and righteousness as the holiness of the saint. Ramdas is not complete without Shivaji. To maintain justice and prevent the strong from despoiling and the weak from being oppressed is the function for which the Kshatriya was created. Therefore, says Sri Krishna in the Mahabharat, God created battle and armour, the sword, the bow and the dagger.[8]*

*
* *

---

* This passage and the preceding one are from unpublished articles which the police seized at the time of Sri Aurobindo's arrest in May, 1908. These two articles were produced as evidence in the Alipore Bomb case, as the prosecution hoped to show that they were seditious and advocated violence to overthrow British rule in India.

*(On May 2, 1908, following a failed assassination attempt on a British judge by revolutionaries belonging to Barin's secret society, Sri Aurobindo was arrested. The British were now confident of having a chance to silence forever "the most dangerous man we have to deal with at present."\* While the famous Alipore Bomb trial went on, Sri Aurobindo, defended by Chittaranjan Das, spent a year in jail, during which he had crucial experiences and revelations; as he wrote later, "Now the inner spiritual life and realisation which had continually been increasing in magnitude and universality and assuming a larger place took him up entirely and his work became a part and result of it and besides far exceeded the service and liberation of the country and fixed itself in an aim, previously only glimpsed, which was world-wide in its bearing and concerned with the whole future of humanity."[11]*

*When after his acquittal on May 6, 1909, Sri Aurobindo came out of the "Alipore ashram," as he called it, the* Bande Mataram *had been stopped by the British, most of the Nationalist leaders jailed, deported or in self-imposed exile, and the few who remained were dispirited —the Nationalist movement was at a low ebb. Sri Aurobindo set about pouring fresh life into it, giving many speeches and starting a new English weekly, the* Karmayogin, *as well as a Bengali weekly, the* Dharma.

*The following excerpts are from the* Karmayogin.*)*

---

\* Thus wrote Lord Minto, the then Viceroy of India, on Sri Aurobindo.[9] Sir Edward Baker, Lieutenant-Governor of Bengal, concurred: "I attribute the spread of seditious doctrines to him personally in a greater degree than to any other single individual in Bengal, or possibly in India."[10]

**May 30, 1909**

*(Extracts from the famous Uttarpara speech.)*

When I approached God at that time [after Sri Aurobindo's return from England], I hardly had a living faith in Him. The agnostic was in me, the atheist was in me, the sceptic was in me and I was not absolutely sure that there was a God at all. I did not feel His presence. Yet something drew me to the truth of the Vedas, the truth of the Gita, the truth of the Hindu religion.* I felt there must be a mighty truth somewhere in this Yoga, a mighty truth in this religion based on the Vedanta. So when I turned to the Yoga and resolved to practise it and find out if my idea was right, I did it in this spirit and with this prayer to Him, "If Thou art, then Thou knowest my heart. Thou knowest that I do not ask for Mukti, I do not ask for anything which others ask for. I ask only for strength to uplift this nation, I ask only to be allowed to live and work for this people whom I love and to whom I pray that I may devote my life." I strove long for the realisation of Yoga and at last to some extent I had it, but in what I most desired I was not satisfied. Then in the seclusion of the jail, of the solitary cell I asked for it again, I said, "Give me Thy Adesh. I do not know what work to do or how to do it. Give me a message." In the communion of Yoga two messages came. The first message said, "I have given you a work and it is to help to uplift this nation. Before long the time will come when you will have to go out of jail; for it is not my will that this time either you should be convicted or that you should pass the time, as others have to do, in suffering for their country. I have called you to work, and that is the Adesh for which you have asked. I give you the Adesh to go forth and

---

* It is important to note that Sri Aurobindo, in the Indian context, uses the word "religion" not in a narrow dogmatic sense, but always in the broader Hindu view of *dharma* (see for instance pp. 50 and 69).

do my work." The second message came and it said, "Something has been shown to you in this year of seclusion, something about which you had your doubts and it is the truth of the Hindu religion. It is this religion that I am raising up before the world, it is this that I have perfected and developed through the Rishis, saints and Avatars, and now it is going forth to do my work among the nations. I am raising up this nation to send forth my word.... When therefore it is said that India shall rise, it is the Sanatan Dharma that shall rise. When it is said that India shall be great, it is the Sanatan Dharma that shall be great. When it is said that India shall expand and extend herself, it is the Sanatan Dharma that shall expand and extend itself over the world. It is for the Dharma and by the Dharma that India exists...."

But what is the Hindu religion? What is this religion which we call Sanatan, eternal? It is the Hindu religion only because the Hindu nation has kept it, because in this Peninsula it grew up in the seclusion of the sea and the Himalayas, because in this sacred and ancient land it was given as a charge to the Aryan race to preserve through the ages.* But it is not circumscribed by the confines of a single country, it does not belong peculiarly and for ever to a bounded part of the world. That which we call the Hindu religion is really the eternal religion, because it is the universal religion which embraces all others. If a religion is not universal, it cannot be eternal. A narrow religion, a sectarian religion, an exclusive religion can live only for a limited time and a limited purpose. This is the one religion that can triumph over materialism by including and anticipating the discoveries of science and the speculations of philosophy. It is the one religion which impresses on mankind the closeness of God to us and embraces in its compass

---

* Sri Aurobindo never subscribed to the absurd division between Aryans and Dravidians: "I regard the so-called Aryans and Dravidians as one homogeneous race," he wrote later in *The Secret of the Veda*. This point will be developed in further passages.

all the possible means by which man can approach God. It is the one religion which insists every moment on the truth which all religions acknowledge that He is in all men and all things and that in Him we move and have our being. It is the one religion which enables us not only to understand and believe this truth but to realise it with every part of our being. It is the one religion which shows the world what the world is, that it is the Lila of Vasudeva. It is the one religion which shows us how we can best play our part in that Lila, its subtlest laws and its noblest rules. It is the one religion which does not separate life in any smallest detail from religion, which knows what immortality is and has utterly removed from us the reality of death....

I said [last year] that this movement is not a political movement and that nationalism is not politics but a religion, a creed, a faith. I say it again today, but I put it in another way. I say no longer that nationalism is a creed, a religion, a faith; I say that it is the Sanatan Dharma which for us is nationalism.... The Sanatan Dharma, that is nationalism. This is the message that I have to speak to you.

\*
\* \*

### June 19, 1909

We have said that *brahmateja* is the thing we need most of all and first of all. In one sense, that means the pre-eminence of religion; but after all, what the Europeans mean by religion is not *brahmateja* which is rather spirituality, the force and energy of thought and action arising from communion with or self-surrender to that within us which rules the world. In that sense we shall use it. This force and energy can be directed to any purpose God desires for us; it is sufficient to knowledge, love or service; it is good for the liberation of an individual soul, the building of a nation or the turning of a tool. It works from within, it works in the power of God, it works with superhuman energy. The reawakening of that force in three hundred millions of men by the means which our past has placed in our hands, that is our object.

The European is proud of his success in divorcing religion from life. Religion, he says, is all very well in its place, but it has nothing to do with politics or science or commerce, which it spoils by its intrusion; it is meant only for Sundays when, if one is English, one puts on black clothes and tries to feel good, and if one is continental, one puts the rest of the week away and amuses oneself.... But after all God does exist and if He exists, you cannot shove Him into a corner and say, "That is your place and as for the world and life it belongs to us." He pervades and returns. Every age of denial is only a preparation for a larger and more comprehensive affirmation.

\*

It is an error, we repeat, to think that spirituality is a thing divorced from life.... It is an error to think that the heights of religion are above the struggles of this world. The recurrent cry of Sri Krishna to Arjuna insists on the struggle; "Fight and overthrow thy opponents!", "Remember me and fight!", "Give up all thy works to me with a heart full of spirituality, and free from craving, free from selfish claims, fight! Let the fever of thy soul pass from thee."

\*

There is a mighty law of life, a great principle of human evolution, a body of spiritual knowledge and experience of which India has always been destined to be guardian, exemplar and missionary. This is the *sanātana dharma*....

The European sets great store by machinery. He seeks to renovate humanity by schemes of society and systems of government; he hopes to bring about the millennium by an act of Parliament. Machinery is of great importance, but only as a working means for the spirit within, the force behind. The nineteenth century in India aspired to political emancipation, social renovation, religious vision and rebirth, but it failed because it adopted Western motives and methods, ignored the spirit, history and destiny of our race and thought that by taking over European education, European machinery, European organisation and equipment we should reproduce in ourselves European prosperity, energy and progress. We of the twentieth century reject the aims, ideals and methods of the anglicised nineteenth, precisely because we accept its experience. We refuse to make an idol of the present; we look before and after, backward to the mighty history of our race, forward to the grandiose history for which that destiny has prepared it....

We say to the nation: "It is God's will that we should be ourselves and not Europe. We have sought to regain life by following the law of another being than our own. We must return and seek the sources of life and strength within ourselves. We must know our past and recover it for the purpose of our future. Our business is to realise ourselves first and to mould everything to the law of India's eternal life and nature...."

We say to the individual and especially to the young who are now arising to do India's work, the world's work, God's work: "You cannot cherish these ideals, still less can you fulfil them if you subject your minds to European ideas or look at life from the material standpoint. Materially you are nothing, spiritually you are everything. It is only the Indian who can believe everything, dare everything, sacrifice everything. First, therefore, become Indians. Recover the patrimony of your forefathers. Recover the Aryan thought, the Aryan discipline, the Aryan character, the Aryan life. Recover the Vedanta, the Gita, the Yoga. Recover them not only in intellect or sentiment but in your lives.... Difficulty and impossibility will vanish from your vocabularies. For it is in the spirit that strength is eternal and you must win back the kingdom of yourselves, the inner Swaraj, before you can win back your outer empire.... Recover the source of all strength in yourselves and all else will be added to you, social soundness, intellectual pre-eminence, political freedom, the mastery of human thought, the hegemony of the world."

\*

We do not fear Mahomedan opposition; so long as it is the honest Swadeshi article and not manufactured in Shillong or Simla,\* we welcome it as a sign of life and aspiration. We do not shun, we desire the awakening of Islam in India even if its first crude efforts are misdirected against ourselves; for all strength, all energy, all action is grist to the mill of the nation-builder. In that faith we are ready, when the time comes for us to meet in the political field, to exchange with the Musulman, just as he chooses, the firm clasp of the brother or the resolute grip of the wrestler....

Of one thing we may be certain, that Hindu-Mahomedan unity cannot be effected by political adjustments or Congress flatteries. It must be sought deeper down, in the heart and in the mind, for where the causes of disunion are, there the remedies must be sought. We shall do well in trying to solve the problem to remember that misunderstanding is the most fruitful cause of our differences, that love compels love and that strength conciliates the strong. We must strive to remove the causes of misunderstanding by a better mutual knowledge and sympathy; we must extend the unfaltering love of the patriot to our Musulman brother, remembering always that in him too Narayana dwells and to him too our Mother has given a permanent place in her bosom; but we must cease to approach him falsely or flatter out of a selfish weakness and cowardice. We believe this to be the only practical way of dealing with the difficulty. As a political question the

---

\* Seats of the British colonial government in India.

Hindu-Mahomedan problem does not interest us at all, as a national problem it is of supreme importance.

*

We shall never lose our fortitude, our courage, our endurance. There are some who think that by lowering our heads the country will escape repression.* That is not my opinion. It is by looking the storm in the face and meeting it with a high courage, fortitude and endurance that the nation can be saved. It is that which the Mother demands from us,—which God demands from us.

*
* *

**June 23, 1909**

*(From a speech at Bakergunj.)*

There are times of great change, times when old landmarks are being upset, when submerged forces are rising, and just as we deal promptly or linger over the solution of these problems, our progress will be rapid or slow, sound or broken.... The problem is put to us one by one, to each nation one by one.... He has shown us the possibility of strength within us, and then He has shown us where the danger, the weakness lies. He is pointing out to us how is it that we may become strong. On us it lies ... to answer the question which God has put to us, and according as we answer on it depends how this movement will progress, what route it will take, and whether it will lead to a swift and sudden salvation, or whether, after so many centuries of tribulation and sufferings there is still a long period of tribulation and suffering before us. God has put the question to us and with us entirely it lies to answer.

*
* *

---

* Since the uprising that followed the partition of Bengal, the Colonial government's repression had become particularly cunning and ruthless.

**June 25, 1909**

*(From a speech at Khulna.)*

The virtue of the Brahmin is a great virtue. You shall not kill. This is what Ahimsa means. If the virtue of Ahimsa comes to the Kshatriya, if you say, "I will not kill," there is no one to protect the country. The happiness of the people will be broken down. Injustice and lawlessness will reign. The virtue becomes a source of misery, and you become instrumental in bringing misery and conflict to the people.

*\* \**

**July 3, 1909**

When confronted with the truths of Hinduism, the experience of deep thinkers and the choice spirits of the race through thousands of years, [the rationalist] shouts "Mysticism, mysticism!" and thinks he has conquered. To him there is order, development, progress, evolution, enlightenment in the history of Europe, but the past of India is an unsightly mass of superstition and ignorance best torn out of the book of human life. These thousands of years of our thought and aspiration are a period of the least importance to us and the true history of our progress only begins with the advent of European education!

*\* \**

**July 17, 1909**

There are particular movements in particular epochs in which the Divine Force manifests itself with supreme power shattering all human calculations, making a mock of the prudence of the careful statesman and the scheming politician, falsifying the prognostications of the scientific analyser and advancing with a vehemence and velocity which is obviously the manifestation of a higher than human force. The intellectual man afterwards tries to trace the reasons for the movement and lay bare the forces that made it possible, but at the time he is utterly at fault, his wisdom is falsified at every step and his science serves him not. These are the times when we say God is in the movement, He is its leader and it must fulfil itself however impossible it may be for man to see the means by which it will succeed.

*
* *

**July 24, 1909**

Terrorism thrives on administrative violence and injustice; that is the only atmosphere in which it can thrive and grow. It sometimes follows the example of indiscriminate violence from above; it sometimes, though very rarely, sets it from below. But the power above which follows the example from below is on the way to committing suicide.

*
* *

**July 31, 1909**

Our ideal is that of Swaraj or absolute autonomy free from foreign control. We claim the right of every nation to live its own life by its own energies according to its own nature and ideals. We reject the claim of aliens to force upon us a civilisation inferior to our own or to keep us out of our inheritance on the untenable ground of a superior fitness. While admitting the stains and defects which long subjection has induced upon our native capacity and energy, we are conscious of that capacity and energy reviving in us.

*
* *

**August 7, 1909**

The future belongs to the young. It is a young and new world which is now under process of development and it is the young who must create it. But it is also a world of truth, courage, justice, lofty aspiration and straightforward fulfilment which we seek to create. For the coward, for the self-seeker, for the talker who goes forward at the beginning and afterwards leaves his fellows in the lurch there is no place in the future of this movement. A brave, frank, clean-hearted, courageous and aspiring youth is the only foundation on which the future nation can be built.... God does not want falterers and flinchers for his work, nor does he want unstable enthusiasts who cannot maintain the energy of their first movements.

*
* *

**August 21, 1909**

The spiritual force within not only creates the future but creates the materials for the future. It is not limited to the existing materials either in their nature or in their quantity. It can transform bad material into good material, insufficient means into abundant means. It was a deep consciousness of this great truth that gave Mazzini the strength to create modern Italy....

It is our hope that ... not only the political circumstances of India be changed but her deeper disease be cured and by a full evocation of her immense stores of moral and spiritual strength that be accomplished for India which Mazzini could not accomplish for Italy, to place her in the head and fore-front of the new world whose birth-throes are now beginning to convulse the Earth.

*
* *

**August 28, 1909**

Strength attracts strength; firm and clear-minded courage commands success and respect; strong and straight dealing can dispense with the methods of dissimulation and intrigue. All these are signs of character and it is only character that can give freedom and greatness to nations.

*

We suppose in a bureaucracy it is inevitable that officials should be masters and be able to inflict inconvenience and loss on the citizen without any means of redress.... If officialdom were to acquire a common sense, the laws of Nature would be sadly contravened.

*
* *

**September 4, 1909**

Every action for instance which may be objectionable to a number of Mahomedans is now liable to be forbidden because it is likely to lead to a breach of the peace, and one is dimly beginning to wonder whether the day may not come when worship in Hindu temples may be forbidden on that valid ground.

*
* *

**September 11, 1909**

Action solves the difficulties which action creates. Inaction can only paralyse and slay.... The errors of life and progress are more exuberant and striking but less fatal than the errors of decay and reaction.

*
* *

## September 18, 1909

The end of a stage of evolution is usually marked by a powerful recrudescence of all that has to go out of the evolution.... The law is the same for the mass as for the individual. The process of human evolution has been seen by the eye of inspired observation to be that of working out the tiger and the ape. The forces of cruelty, lust, mischievous destruction, pain-giving, folly, brutality, ignorance were once rampant·in humanity, they had full enjoyment; then by the growth of religion and philosophy they began in periods of satiety such as the beginning of the Christian era in Europe to be partly replaced, partly put under control. As is the law of such things, they have always reverted again with greater or less virulence and sought with more or less success to re-establish themselves. Finally, in the nineteenth century it seemed for a time as if some of these forces had, for the time at least, exhausted themselves and the hour for *samyama* [rejection] and gradual dismissal from the evolution had really arrived. Such hopes always recur and in the end they are likely to bring about their own fulfilment, but before that happens another recoil is inevitable. We see plenty of signs of it in the reeling back into the beast which is in progress in Europe and America behind the fair outside of Science, progress, civilisation and humanitarianism, and we are likely to see more signs of it in the era that is coming upon us.

\*
\* \*

## September 25, 1909

The debasement of our mind, character and tastes by a grossly commercial, materialistic and insufficient European education is a fact on which the young Nationalism has always insisted. The practical destruction of our artistic perceptions and the plastic skill and fineness of eye and hand which once gave our productions pre-eminence, distinction and mastery of the European markets, is also a thing accomplished. Most vital of all, the spiritual and intellectual divorce from the past which the present schools and universities have effected, has beggared the nation of the originality, high aspiration and forceful energy which can alone make a nation free and great. To reverse the process and recover what we have lost, is undoubtedly the first object to which we ought to devote ourselves. And as the loss of originality, aspiration and energy was the most vital of all these losses, so their recovery should be our first and most important objective. The primary aim of the prophets of Nationalism was to rid the nation of the idea that the future was limited by the circumstances of the present, that because temporary causes had brought us low and made us weak, low therefore must be our aims and weak our methods. They pointed the mind of the people to a great and splendid destiny, not in some distant millennium but in the comparatively near future.... To raise the mind, character and tastes of the people, to recover the ancient nobility of temper, the strong Aryan character and the high Aryan outlook, the perceptions which made earthly life beautiful and wonderful, and the magnificent spiritual experiences, realisations and aspirations which made us the deepest-hearted, deepest-thoughted and most delicately profound in life of all the peoples of the earth, is the task next in importance and urgency....

We must remember also why the degradation and denationalisation, "the mighty evil in our souls" of which the writer* complains, came into being. A painful but necessary work had to be done, and because the English nation were the fittest instrument for his purpose, God led them all over those thousands of miles of alien Ocean, gave strength to their hearts and subtlety to their brains, and set them up in

---

* Sri Aurobindo is referring to "The Message of the East," an article written by A. K. Coomaraswamy in *The Modern Review*.

India to do His work, which they have been doing faithfully, if blindly, ever since and are doing at the present moment. The spirit and ideals of India had come to be confined in a mould which, however beautiful, was too narrow and slender to bear the mighty burden of our future. When that happens, the mould has to be broken and even the ideal lost for a while, in order to be recovered free of constraint and limitation.... We must not cabin the expanding and aggressive spirit of India in temporary forms which are the creation of the last few hundred years. That would be a vain and disastrous endeavour. The mould is broken; we must remould in larger outlines and with a richer content. For the work of destruction England was best fitted by her stubborn individuality and by that very commercialism and materialism which made her the anti-type in temper and culture of the race she governed. She was chosen too for the unrivalled efficiency and skill with which she has organised an individualistic and materialistic democracy. We had to come to close quarters with that democratic organisation, draw it into ourselves and absorb the democratic spirit and methods so that we might rise beyond them.... We have to throw away the individualism and materialism and keep the democracy. We have to solve for the human race the problem of harmonising and spiritualising its impulses towards liberty, equality and fraternity.

*<br>* *

**October 2, 1909**

An imitation of the forms and workings of the old Congress is also inadvisable. We were never satisfied with those forms and that working. The three days' show [i.e. the Congress sessions], the excessively festal aspect of the occasion, the monstrous preponderance of speech and resolution-passing over action and work, the want of true democratic rule and order, the weary waste of formal oratory without any practical use or object, the incapacity of the assembly for grappling with the real problems of our national existence and progress, the anxiety to avoid public discussion which is the life-breath of democratic politics, these and many other defects made the Congress in our view an instrument ill-made, wasteful of money and energy, and the centre of a false conception of political deliberation and action. If we imitate the Congress, we shall contract all the faults of the Congress.

\*
\* \*

### November 6, 1909

> *(In 1909, the Morley-Minto Reform Scheme gave Indian Muslims a separate electorate to "reformed" legislative councils, in effect encouraging them to assert their separate identity.)*

The question of separate representation for the Mahomedan community is one of those momentous issues raised in haste by a statesman unable to appreciate the forces with which he is dealing, which bear fruit no man expected and least of all the ill-advised Frankenstein who was first responsible for its creation. The common belief among Hindus is that the Government have decided to depress the Hindu element in the Indian people by raising the Mahomedan element, and ensure a perpetual preponderance in their own favour by leaning on a Mahomedan vote purchased by a system of preference. The denials of high-placed officials, who declare that it is only out of a careful consideration for the rights and interests of minorities that they have made special Mahomedan representation an essential feature of the Reform Scheme, have not convinced a single Hindu mind; for the obvious retort is that it is only one minority which is specially cared for and this special care is extended to it even in provinces where it is in a large majority. No provision at all has been made for the safeguarding of Hindu minorities, for the Parsis, the Sikhs, the Christians and other sections which may reasonably declare that they too are Indians and citizens of the Empire no less than the Mahomedans....

Our own attitude is clear. We will have no part or lot in reforms which give no popular majority, no substantive control, no opportunity for Indian capacity and statesmanship, no seed of democratic expansion. We will not for a moment accept separate electorates or separate representation, not because we are opposed to a large Mahomedan influence in popular assemblies when they come but because we will be no party to a distinction which recognises Hindu and Mahomedan as permanently separate political units and thus precludes the growth of a single and indivisible Indian nation. We oppose any such attempt at division whether it comes from an embarassed Government seeking for political support or from an embittered Hindu community allowing the passions of the moment to obscure their vision of the future.

*

Dr. U. N. Mukherji recently published a very interesting brochure in which he tried to prove that the Hindus were a dying race and would do well to imitate the social freedom and equality of the still increasing Mahomedans....

The real truth is that, owing to an immense transition being effected under peculiarly unfavourable conditions, both communities, but chiefly the more progressive Hindu, are in a critical stage in which various deep-seated maladies have come to the surface, with effects of an inevitable though lamentable character. None of these maladies is mortal and the race is not dying. But the knife of the surgeon is needed and it is to the remedy rather than the diagnosis that attention should be pointedly directed. The mere decline in the rate of increase is in itself nothing. It is a phenomenon which one now sees becoming more and more marked all the world over and it is only countries backward in development and education which keep up the old rate of increase. The unfit tend to multiply, the fit to be limited in propagation. This is an abnormal state of things which indicates something wrong in modern civilisation. But, whatever the malady is, it is not peculiar to Hindus or to India, but a world-wide disease.

\*

The Mahomedans base their separateness and their refusal to regard themselves as Indians first and Mahomedans afterwards on the existence of great Mahomedan nations to which they feel themselves more akin, in spite of our common birth and blood, than to us. Hindus have no such resource. For good or evil, they are bound to the soil and to the soil alone. They cannot deny their Mother, neither can they mutilate her. Our ideal therefore is an Indian Nationalism, largely Hindu in its spirit and traditions, because the Hindu made the land and the people and persists, by the greatness of his past, his civilisation and his culture and his invincible virility, in holding it, but wide enough also to include the Moslem and his culture and traditions and absorb them into itself.

\*
\* \*

**November 20, 1909**

Not only class, as was formerly the case, but creed has been made the basis of representation [in the Morley-Minto reforms] and, therefore, unless the Hindus have the strength of mind to boycott a system which creates a distinction insulting as well as injurious to the community, this measure, while giving us not an atom of self-government, will be a potent engine for dividing the nation into two hostile interests and barring the way towards the unity of India. Formerly, there were only two classes in India, the superior European and the inferior Indian; now there will be three, the supreme European, the superior Mahomedan and the inferior Hindu. This is loss number one, and it is no small one, to the Mahomedan no less than the Hindu. The official of course gains.

*

In India ... we have been cut off by a mercenary and soulless education from all our ancient roots of culture and tradition....

The value attached by ancients to music, art and poetry has become almost unintelligible to an age bent on depriving life of its meaning by turning earth into a sort of glorified ant-heap or beehive.

...

The future is mightier than the past and evolution proceeds relentlessly in its course trampling to pieces all that it no longer needs. Those who fight against her fight against the will of God, against a decree written from of old, and are already defeated and slain in the *kāranajagat*, the world of types and causes where Nature fixes everything before she works it out in the visible world.

*
* *

**November 27, 1909**

A purely scientific education tends to make thought keen and clear-sighted within certain limits, but narrow, hard and cold.... Man intellectually developed, mighty in scientific knowledge and the mastery of the gross and subtle nature, using the elements as his servants and the world as his footstool, but underdeveloped in heart and spirit, becomes only an inferior kind of *asura* using the powers of a demigod to satisfy the nature of an animal.

*
* *

**December 11, 1909**

Between them music, art and poetry are a perfect education for the soul; they make and keep its movements purified, self-controlled, deep and harmonious. These, therefore, are agents which cannot profitably be neglected by humanity on its onward march or degraded to the mere satisfaction of sensuous pleasure which will disintegrate rather than build the character. They are, when properly used, great educating, edifying and civilising forces.

\*
\* \*

**December 25, 1909**

The system of education which, instead of keeping artistic training apart as a privilege for a few specialists frankly introduces it as a part of culture no less necessary than literature or science, will have taken a great step forward in the perfection of national education and the general diffusion of a broad-based human culture. It is not necessary that every man should be an artist. It is necessary that every man should have his artistic faculty developed, his taste trained, his sense of beauty and insight into form and colour and that which is expressed in form and colour, made habitually active, correct and sensitive. It is necessary that those who create, whether in great things or small, whether in the unusual masterpieces of art and genius or in the small common things of use that surround a man's daily life, should be habituated to produce and the nation habituated to expect the beautiful in preference to the ugly, the noble in preference to the vulgar, the fine in preference to the crude, the harmonious in preference to the gaudy. A nation surrounded daily by the beauful, noble, fine and harmonious becomes that which it is habituated to contemplate and realises the fullness of the expanding Spirit in itself....

In India the revival of a truly national Art is already an accomplished fact and the masterpieces of the school can already challenge comparison with the best work of other countries.* Under such circumstances it is unpardonable that the crude formal teaching of English schools and the vulgar commercial aims and methods of the West should subsist in our midst. The country has yet to evolve a system of education which shall be really national. The taint of Occidental ideals and alien and unsuitable methods has to be purged out of our minds, and nowhere more than in the teaching which should be the foundation of intellectual and aesthetic renovation. The spirit of old Indian Art must be revived, the inspiration and directness of vision which even now subsists among the possessors of the ancient traditions, the inborn skill and taste of the race, the dexterity of the Indian hand and the intuitive gaze of the Indian eye must be recovered and the whole nation lifted again to the high level of the ancient culture—and higher.

*
* *

**Undated**

We of today have been overpowered by the European tradition as interpreted by the English, the least artistic of civilised nations. We have therefore come to make on a picture the same demand as on a photograph,—the reproduction of the thing as the eye sees it.... The conception that Art exists not to copy, but for the sake of a deeper truth and vision, and we must seek in it not the object but God in the object, not things but the soul of things, seems to have vanished for a while from the Indian consciousness....

---

* Sri Aurobindo is referring in particular to the remarkable artistic awakening which Bengal witnessed at the end of the nineteenth century, with the Tagore family providing its most talented leaders. This revival, however, could not resist the utilitarian onslaught and started fading away in the 1930s.

Indian Art demands of the artist the power of communion with the soul of things, the sense of spiritual taking precedence of the sense of material beauty, and fidelity to the deeper vision within....

*
* *

### January 1, 1910

It is foolish to expect men to make great sacrifices while discouraging their hope and enthusiasm. It is not intellectual recognition of duty that compels sustained self-sacrifice in masses of men; it is hope, it is the lofty ardour of a great cause, it is the enthusiasm of a noble and courageous effort.

*
* *

### January 15, 1910

A bureaucracy is always inclined to be arrogant, self-sufficient, self-righteous and unsympathetic, to ignore the abuses with which it abounds....

*
* *

### Early 1910

There is no word so plastic and uncertain in its meaning as the word religion. The word is European.... The average Christian believes that the Bible is God's book, but ordinarily he does not consider anything in God's book binding on him in practice except to believe in God and go to Church once a week; the rest is only meant for the exceptionally pious. On the whole, therefore, to believe in God, to believe that He wrote a book,—only one book in all these ages,—and to go to Church on Sunday is the minimum of religion in Europe; on these essentials piety and morality may supervene and deepen the meaning.

Religion in India is a still more plastic term and may mean anything from the heights of Yoga to strangling your fellow-man and relieving him of the worldly goods he may happen to be carrying with him. It would therefore take too long to enumerate everything that can be included in Indian religion. Briefly, however, it is *dharma* or living religiously, the whole life being governed by religion. But again what is living religiously? It means, in ordinary practice, living according to authority. The authority generally accepted is the Shastra; but when one studies the Shastra and Indian life side by side, one finds that the two have very little to do with each other; the Indian governs his life not by the Shastra but by custom and the opinion of the nearest Brahmin. In practice this resolves itself into certain observances and social customs of which he understands neither the spiritual meaning nor the practical utility. To venerate the Scriptures without knowing them and to obey custom in their place; to reverence all Brahmins whether they are venerable or despicable; to eat nothing cooked by a social inferior; to marry one's daughter before puberty and one's son as soon as possible after it; to keep women ignorant and domestically useful; to bathe scrupulously and go through certain fixed ablutions; to eat on the floor and not at a table; to do one's devotions twice a day without understanding them; to observe a host of meaningless minutiae in one's daily conduct; to keep the Hindu holidays, when an image is set up, worshipped and thrown away, —this in India is the minimum of religion. This is glorified as Hinduism and the Sanatana Dharma. If, in addition, a man has emotional or ecstatic piety, he is a Bhakta; if he can talk fluently about the Veda, Upanishads, Darshanas and Puranas, he is a Jnani. If he puts on a yellow robe and does nothing, he is a *tyāgī* or *sannyāsin*. The latter is liberated from the ordinary dharma, but only if he does nothing but beg and vegetate. All work must be according to custom and the Brahmin. The one superiority of average Indian religion is that it does really reverence the genuine Bhakta or Sannyasin provided he does not come with too strange a garb or too revolutionary an aspect. The European almost invariably sets him down as a charlatan, professional religionist, idle drone or religious maniac.

...

The average Hindu is right in his conception of religion as dharma, to live according to holy rule; but the holy rule is not a mass of fugitive and temporary customs, but this, to live for God in oneself and others and not for oneself only, to make the whole life a sadhana the object of which is to realise the Divine in the world by work, love and knowledge.[12]

*
* *

*(Early in 1910, the Colonial government took advantage of a few terrorist acts to stamp out all opposition, arrest and deport Nationalist leaders and pass increasingly tyrannical laws. There remained in the field the impotent Moderates on the one hand, and on the other fruitless and directionless violence. Simultaneously, there were more pressing portents that the government had finally decided to arrest Sri Aurobindo again, deport him under its draconian laws, and silence the* Karmayogin. *In mid-February, following news of an impending arrest, Sri Aurobindo received an Adesh to go to Chandernagore, then under French government. Leaving the* Karmayogin *office at once, he reached Chandernagore the next morning, where he remained for a month and a half, immersed in sadhana. Most of the following extracts are from articles he had written before leaving, or perhaps sent from Chandernagore to the* Karmayogin, *which he had left in the charge of Sister Nivedita. At the end of March, he received a second Adesh to go to Pondicherry. The last issue of the* Karmayogin *came out on April 2, 1910.)*

## February 19, 1910

Life creates institutions; institutions do not create, but express and preserve life. This is a truth we are too apt to forget. The Europeans and especially our Gurus, the English, attach an exaggerated importance to machinery, because their own machinery has been so successful, their organisation so strong and triumphant. In the conceit of this success they imagine that their machinery is the only machinery and that the adoption of their organisation by foreign peoples is all that is needed for perfect social and political felicity.... To take over those institutions and think that they will magically develop European virtues, force and robustness, or the vivid and vigorous life of Europe, is as if a man were to steal another's coat and think to take over with it his character. Have not indeed many of us thought by masquerading in the amazing garb which nineteenth century Europe developed, to become so many brown Englishmen? This curious conjuring trick did not work; hatted, coated and pantalooned, we still kept the Chaddar and the Dhoty in our characters. The fond attempt to become great, enlightened and civilised by borrowing European institutions will be an equally disastrous failure.

...

But in Europe and India alike we seem to stand on the threshold of a vast revolution, political, social and religious. Whatever nation now is the first to solve the problems which are threatening to hammer Governments, creeds, societies into pieces all the world over, will lead the world in the age that is coming. It is our ambition that India should be that nation. But in order that she should be what we wish, it is necessary that she should be capable of unsparing revolution. She must have the courage of her past knowledge and the immensity of soul that will measure itself with her future.

*

Men see the waves, they hear the rumour and the thousand voices and by these they judge the course of the future and the heart of God's intention; but in nine cases out of ten they misjudge. Therefore it is said that in history it is always the unexpected that happens. But it would not be the unexpected if men could turn their eyes from superficies and look into substance, if they accustomed themselves to put aside appearances and penetrate beyond them to the secret and disguised reality, if they ceased listening to the noise of life and listened rather to its silence.

*
* *

**February 26, 1910**

The attempt to make boys moral and religious by the teaching of moral and religious text-books is a vanity and a delusion, precisely because the heart is not the mind and to instruct the mind does not necessarily improve the heart.... The danger of moral text-books is that they make the thinking of high things mechanical and artificial, and whatever is mechanical and artificial is inoperative for good....

You can impose a certain discipline on children, dress them into a certain mould, lash them into a desired path, but unless you can get their hearts and natures on your side the conformity to this imposed rule becomes a hypocritical and heartless, a conventional, often a cowardly compliance....

The first rule of moral training is to suggest and invite, not command or impose. The best method of suggestion is by personal example, daily converse and the books read from day to day. These books should contain, for the younger student, the lofty example of the past given, not as moral lessons, but as things of supreme human interest, and, for the elder student, the great thoughts of great souls, the passages of literature which set fire to the highest emotions and prompt the highest ideals and aspirations, the records of history and biography which exemplify the living of those great thoughts, noble emotions and aspiring ideals. This is a kind of good company, *satsanga*, which can seldom fail to have effect so long as sententious sermonising is avoided, and becomes of the highest effect if the personal life of the teacher is itself moulded by the great things he places before his pupils. It cannot, however, have full force unless the young life is given opportunity, within its limited sphere, of embodying in action the moral impulses which rise within it.

*

The events that sway the world are often the results of trivial circumstances. When immense changes and irresistible movements are in progress, it is astonishing how a single event, often a chance event, will lead to a train of circumstances that alter the face of a country or the world. At such times a slight turn this way or that produces results out of all proportion to the cause. It is on such occasions that we feel most vividly the reality of a Power which disposes of events and defeats the calculations of men. The end of many things is brought about by the sudden act of a single individual. A world vanishes, another is created almost at a touch. Certainty disappears and we begin to realise what the *pralaya* of the Hindus, the passage from one age to another, really means and how true is the idea that it is by rapid transitions long-prepared changes are induced. Such a change now impends all over the world, and in almost all countries events are happening, the final results of which the actors do not foresee. Small incidents pass across the surface of great countries and some of them pass and are forgotten, others precipitate the future.

*
* *

**March 5, 1910**

A very remarkable feature of modern training which has been subjected in India to a *reductio ad absurdum* is the practice of teaching by snippets. A subject is taught a little at a time, in conjunction with a host of others, with the result that what might be well learnt in a single year is badly learned in seven and the boy goes out ill-equipped, served with imperfect parcels of knowledge, master of none of the great departments of human knowledge....

The old system was to teach one or two subjects well and thoroughly and then proceed to others, and certainly it was a more rational system than the modern. If it did not impart so much varied information, it built up a deeper, nobler and more real culture. Much of the shallowness, discursive lightness and fickle mutability of the average modern mind is due to the vicious principle of teaching by snippets. The one defect that can be alleged against the old system was that the subject earliest learned might fade from the mind of the student while he was mastering his later studies. But the excellent training given to the memory by the ancients obviated the incidence of this defect. In the future education we need not bind ourselves either by the ancient or the modern system, but select only the most perfect and rapid means of mastering knowledge.

In defence of the modern system it is alleged that the attention of children is easily tired and cannot be subjected to the strain of long application to a single subject. The frequent change of subject gives rest to the mind. The question naturally arises: are the children of modern times then so different from the ancients, and, if so, have we not made them so by discouraging prolonged concentration?... A child of seven or eight, and that is the earliest permissible age for the commencement of any regular kind of study, is capable of a good deal of concentration if he is interested. Interest is, after all, the basis of concentration. We make his lessons supremely uninteresting and repellent to the child, a harsh compulsion the basis of teaching and then complain of his restless inattention! The substitution of a natural self-education by the child for the present unnatural system will remove this objection of inability. A child, like a man, if he is interested, much prefers to get to the end of his subject rather than leave it unfinished. To lead him on step by step, interesting and absorbing him in each as it comes, until he has mastered his subject is the true art of teaching.

. . .

The mother-tongue is the proper medium of education and therefore the first energies of the child should be directed to the thorough mastering of the medium. Almost every child has an imagination, an instinct for words, a dramatic faculty, a wealth of idea and fancy. These should be interested in the literature and history of the nation. Instead of stupid and

dry spelling and reading books, looked on as a dreary and
ungrateful task, he should be introduced by rapidly progressive stages to the most interesting parts of his own literature
and the life around him and behind him, and they should be
put before him in such a way as to attract and appeal to the
qualities of which I have spoken. All other study at this
period should be devoted to the perfection of the mental
functions and the moral character. A foundation should be
laid at this time for the study of history, science, philosophy,
art, but not in an obtrusive and formal manner. Every child
is a lover of interesting narrative, a hero-worshipper and a
patriot. Appeal to these qualities in him and through them let
him master without knowing it the living and human parts of
his nation's history. Every child is an inquirer, an investigator,
analyser, a merciless anatomist. Appeal to those qualities in
him and let him acquire without knowing it the right temper
and the necessary fundamental knowledge of the scientist.
Every child has an insatiable intellectual curiosity and turn
for metaphysical enquiry. Use it to draw him on slowly to an
understanding of the world and himself. Every child has the
gift of imitation and a touch of imaginative power. Use it to
give him the ground-work of the faculty of the artist....

Teaching by snippets must be relegated to the lumber-room
of dead sorrows.

*
\* \*

**March 26, 1910**

The work that was begun at Dakshineshwar is far from
finished, it is not even understood. That which Vivekananda
received and strove to develop, has not yet materialised. The
truth of the future that Bijoy Goswami hid within himself,
has not yet been revealed utterly to his disciples. A less
discrete revelation prepares, a more concrete force manifests,
but where it comes, when it comes, none knoweth.

*
\* \*

*(The following extracts are from* Epistles from Abroad, *written to an imaginary correspondent in India. Sri Aurobindo wrote these* Epistles *early in 1910 and probably intended to publish them in the* Karmayogin, *but could not owing to his abrupt departure from Calcutta. Some of the last extracts are from Epistles he wrote shortly after his arrival at Pondicherry.)*

Dearly beloved,

...

Was life always so trivial, always so vulgar, always so loveless, pale and awkward as the Europeans have made it? This well-appointed comfort oppresses me, this perfection of machinery will not allow the soul to remember that it is not itself a machine.

Is this then the end of the long march of human civilisation, this spiritual suicide, this quiet petrifaction of the soul into matter? Was the successful businessman that grand culmination of manhood toward which evolution was striving? After all, if the scientific view is correct, why not? An evolution that started with the protoplasm and flowered in the ourang-outang and the chimpanzee, may well rest satisfied with having created hat, coat and trousers, the British Aristocrat, the American Capitalist and the Parisian Apache. For these, I believe, are the chief triumphs of the European enlightenment to which we bow our heads. For these Augustus created Europe, Charlemagne refounded civilisation, Louis XIV regulated society, Napoleon systematised the French Revolution. For these Goethe thought, Shakespeare imagined and created, St. Francis loved, Christ was crucified. What a bankruptcy! What a beggary of things that were rich and noble!

Europe boasts of her science and its marvels. But an Indian cannot content himself with asking like Voltaire, as the supreme question, "What have you invented?" His glance is at the soul; it is that into which he is accustomed to enquire. To the braggart intellect of Europe he is bound to reply, "I am not interested in what you know, I am interested in what you are. With all your discoveries and inventions, what have you become? Your enlightenment is great,—but what are these strange creatures that move about in the electric light you have installed and imagine that they are human?" Is it a great gain for the human intellect to have grown more acute and discerning, if the human soul dwindles?

But Science does not admit the existence of soul. The soul, it says, is only an organised republic of animalcules, and it is in the mould of that idea Europe has recast herself;—that is what the European nations are becoming, organised republics of animalcules,—very intelligent, very methodical, very wonderful talking and reasoning animalcules but still animalcules. Not what the race set out to be, creatures made in the image of the Almighty, gods that having fallen from heaven remember and strive to recover their heritage. Man in Europe is descending steadily from the human level and approximating to the ant and the hornet. The process is not complete but it is progressing apace, and if nothing stops the debacle, we may hope to see its culmination in this twentieth century. After all our superstitions were better than this enlightenment, our social abuses less murderous to the hopes of the race than this social perfection.

It is a very pleasant inferno they have created in Europe, a hell not of torments but of pleasures, of lights and carriages, of balls and dances and suppers, of theatres and cafés and music-halls, of libraries and clubs and Academies, of National Galleries and Exhibitions, of factories, shops, banks and Stock Exchanges. But it is hell all the same, not the heaven of which the saints and the poets dreamed, the new Jerusalem, the golden city. London and New York are the holy cities of the new religion, Paris its golden Paradise of Pleasure.

It is not with impunity that men decide to believe that they are animals and God does not exist. For what we believe, that we become. The animal lives by a routine arranged for him by Nature; his life is devoted to the satisfaction of his instincts bodily, vital and emotional, and he satisfies himself mechanically, by a regular response to the working of those instincts. Nature has regularised everything for him and provided the machinery. Man in Europe arranges his own routine, invents his own machinery, and adds to the needs of which he is a slave, the intellectual. But there will soon be no other difference.

System, organisation, machinery have attained their perfection. Bondage has been carried to its highest expression, and from a passion for organising external liberty Europe is slaying her spiritual freedom. When the inner freedom is gone, the external liberty will follow it, and a social tyranny more terrible, inquisitorial and relentless than any that caste ever organised in India, will take its place. The process has already begun. The shell of external liberty remains, the core is already being eaten away. Because he is still free to gratify his senses and enjoy himself, the European thinks himself free. He does not know what teeth are gnawing into the heart of his liberty.[13]

*

It will be well when every Indian, instead of taking a waxlike stamp from his foreign surroundings, is able to carry India with him wherever he goes. For that will mean that India is destined to conquer and place her stamp upon the whole world.[14]

*

For my part I see failure written large over all the splendid and ostentatious achievements of Europe. Her costliest experiments, her greatest expenditure of intellectual and moral force have led to the swiftest exhaustion of creative activity, the completest bankruptcy of moral elevation and discouraging of man's once infinite hope. When one considers how many and swift her bankruptcies have been, the imagination is appalled by the swiftness of this motor ride to ruin. The bankruptcy of the ideas of the French Revolution, the bankruptcy of utilitarian Liberalism, the bankruptcy of national altruism, the bankruptcy of humanitarianism, the bankruptcy of religious faith, the bankruptcy of political sincerity, the bankruptcy of true commercial honesty, the bankruptcy of the personal sense of honour, how swiftly they have all followed on each other or raced with each other for precedence and kept at least admirable pace. Only her many-sided science with its great critical and analytical power and all the contrivances that come of analysis, is still living and keeps her erect. There remains that last bankruptcy yet to come and when that is once over, what will be left? Already I see a dry rot begun in this its most sapful and energetic part. The firm materialism which was its life and protection, is beginning also to go bankrupt, and one sees nothing but craze and fantasy ready to take its place.

...

A thousand newspapers vulgarise knowledge, debase aesthetical appreciation, democratise success and make impossible all that was once unusual and noble. The man of letters has become a panderer to the intellectual appetites of a mob or stands aloof in the narrowness of a coterie. There is plenty of brilliance everywhere, but one searches in vain for a firm foundation, the power or the solidity of knowledge. The select seek paradox in order to distinguish themselves from the herd; a perpetual reiteration of some startling novelty can alone please the crowd.... Of all literary forms the novel only has still some genius and even that is perishing of the modern curse of overproduction.

Learning and scholarship are unendingly active over the dead corpse of creative power as in Alexandria and with the later Romans before the great darkness.... Yesterday's opinion is today exploded and discarded, new fireworks of theory, generalisation and speculation take the place of the old, and to this pyrotechnic rushing in a circle they give the name of progress....

In a word, the whole of Europe is now a magnified Alexandria, brilliant forms with a perishing soul in imitation of the forms of health, feverish activity with no capital but the energy of the sickbed. One has to concede however that it is not altogether sterile, for all Europe and America pullulate with ever multiplying machinery.[15]

\*

These hollow worm-eaten outsides of Hinduism crumbling so sluggishly, so fatally to some sudden and astonishing dissolution, do not frighten me. Within them I find the soul of a civilisation alive, though sleeping. I see upon it the consoling sentence of God, "Because thou hast believed in me, therefore thou shalt live and not perish." Also, I look through the garnished outsides, gaudy, not beautiful, pretentious, not great, boastful, not secure, of this vaunting, aggressive, dominant Europe and I have seen written on the heart of its civilisation a sentence of death and mounting already from the heart to the brain an image of annihilation....

It is not in noble figures that she presents herself to my imagination, this sole enlightened continent, it is not fear or respect that they awaken in my mind, these civilised superior nations. I see a little girl wearing a new frock and showing herself off to Mamma and all the world, unable to conceal her pride and delight in the thought that never was a frock so new and nice or a little girl so pretty,—never was and never will be! I think of a very small boy to whom somebody has given a very big cane—one can see him brandishing it, executing now and then an exultant war-dance, tormenting, tyrannising over and plundering of their little belongings all the smaller boys he can get within his cane's reach, not displeased if they show a little fight so that he can exhibit his heroic strength of arm by punishing them. And then he adorns himself with glittering Victoria crosses and calls on all his associates to admire his gallant and his daredevil courage. Sometimes it reminds me of an old man, a man very early old, still strong in his decrepitude, garrulous, well-informed, luxurious, arrogant, intelligent, still busy toddling actively from place to place, looking into this, meddling in that, laying down the law dogmatically on every point under the sun; and through it all the clutch already nearing the brain, the shaking of the palsy already foreshadowed in tremulous movement and uncertain nerve. Very true, Europe, your frock is the cleanest and newest, for the present, your stick the biggest, your war-dance a very frightening spectacle,—frightening even to yourselves—with Krupp and Mauser and machine gun what else should it be, you are indeed for a while the robust, enlightened oldster you seem. But afterwards. Well, afterwards there will be a newer frock, a bigger stick, a war-dance much more terrible and a real Titan grasping at the earth for his own instead of the sham.[16]

\* \*
\*

# II

## 1910 — 1922

*(On April 4, 1910, Sri Aurobindo, still wanted by the British, reached Pondicherry clandestinely. A third charge of sedition against him, for an article in the* Karmayogin, *failed in his absence. For several years he was going to live in this French colony as a fugitive, with spies and rumours hovering about him and his small group of companions.*

*For some time Sri Aurobindo thought of returning to British India, but he soon saw that "enough had been done to change the whole face of Indian politics and the whole spirit of the Indian people to make independence its aim," as he wrote later. "His own personal intervention in politics would therefore no longer be indispensable. Apart from all this, the magnitude of the spiritual work set before him became more and more clear to him, and he saw that the concentration of all his energies on it was necessary." But Sri Aurobindo's retirement from political activity "did not mean, as most people supposed, that he had retired into some height of spiritual experience devoid of any further interest in the world or in the fate of India."[17]*

*The following excerpts are from letters, articles and essays; many of the latter appeared in the* Arya, *an English monthly Sri Aurobindo published from 1914 to 1921, in which he wrote most of his important works.)*

## 1910-1912

We have, most of us, our chosen explanation of this dolorous phenomenon [of the decline of Indian civilisation]. The patriot attributes our decline to the ravages of foreign invasion and the benumbing influences of foreign rule; the disciple of European materialism finds out the enemy, the evil, the fount and origin of all our ills, in our religion and its time-honoured social self-expression. Such explanations, like most human thoughts, have their bright side of truth as well as their obscure side of error; but they are not, in any case, the result of impartial thinking. Man may be, as he has been defined, a reasoning animal, but it is necessary to add that he is, for the most part, a very badly reasoning animal. He does not ordinarily think for the sake of finding out the truth, but much more for the satisfaction of his mental preferences and emotional tendencies; his conclusions spring from his preferences, prejudices and passions; and his reasoning and logic paraded to justify them are only a specious process or a formal mask for his covert approach to an upshot previously necessitated by his heart or by his temperament. When we are awakened from our modern illusions, as we have been awakened from our mediaeval superstitions, we shall find that the intellectual conclusions of the rationalist, for all their pomp and protest of scrupulous enquiry, were as much dogmas as those former dicta of Pope and theologian, which confessed without shame their simple basis in the negation of reason.... It is always best, therefore, to scrutinise very narrowly those bare, trenchant explanations which so easily satisfy the pugnacious animal in our intellect; when we have admitted that small part of the truth on which they seize, we should always look for the large part which they have missed.

. . .

Few societies have been so tamasic, so full of inertia and contentment in increasing narrowness as Indian society in later times; few have been so eager to preserve themselves in inertia. Few therefore have attached so great an importance to authority. Every detail of our life has been fixed for us by Shastra and custom, every detail of our thought by Scripture and its commentators,—but much oftener by the commentators than by Scripture. Only in one field, that of individual spiritual experience, have we cherished the ancient freedom and originality out of which our past greatness sprang; it is from some new movement in this inexhaustible source that every fresh impulse and rejuvenated strength has arisen. Otherwise we should long ago have been in the grave where dead nations lie, with Greece and Rome of the Caesars, with Esarhaddon* and the Chosroes**....

The result of this well-meaning bondage [to the outer forms of Hinduism] has been an increasing impoverishment of the Indian intellect, once the most gigantic and original in the world. Hence a certain incapacity, atrophy, impotence have marked our later activities even at their best. The most striking instance is our continued helplessness in the face of the new conditions and new knowledge imposed on us by recent European contact. We have tried to assimilate, we have tried to reject, we have tried to select; but we have not been able to do any of these things successfully. Successful assimilation depends on mastery; but we have not mastered European conditions and knowledge, rather we have been seized, subjected and enslaved by them. Successful rejection is possible only if we have intelligent possession of that which we wish to keep. Our rejection too must be an intelligent rejection; we must reject because we have understood, not because we have failed to understand. But our Hinduism, our old culture are precisely the possessions we have cherished with the least intelligence; throughout the whole range of our life we do things without knowing why we do them,

---

* One of the last Assyrian kings in the seventh century BC.
** Members of the last dynasty of native rulers of Persia, the Sassanids, who ruled from the third to the seventh century AD, until the Mahomedan conquests engulfed Persia.

we believe things without knowing why we believe them, we assert things without knowing what right we have to assert them,—or, at most, it is because some book or some Brahmin enjoins it, because Shankara thinks it, or because someone has so interpreted something that he asserts to be a fundamental Scripture of our religion. Nothing is our own, nothing native to our intelligence, all is derived. As little have we understood the new knowledge; we have only understood what the Europeans want us to think about themselves and their modern civilisation. Our English culture—if culture it can be called—has increased tenfold the evil of our dependence instead of remedying it.

...

How shall we recover our lost intellectual freedom and elasticity? By reversing, for a time at least, the process by which we lost it, by liberating our minds in all subjects from the thraldom to authority. That is not what reformers and the Anglicised require of us. They ask us, indeed, to abandon authority, to revolt against custom and superstition, to have free and enlightened minds. But they mean by these sounding recommendations that we should renounce the authority of Sayana for the authority of Max Müller, the Monism of Shankara for the Monism of Haeckel, the written Shastra for the unwritten law of European social opinion, the dogmatism of Brahmin Pandits for the dogmatism of European scientists, thinkers and scholars. Such a foolish exchange of servitude can receive the assent of no self-respecting mind. Let us break our chains, venerable as they are, but let it be in order to be free,—in the name of truth, not in the name of Europe. It would be a poor bargain to exchange our old Indian illuminations, however dark they may have grown to us, for a derivative European enlightenment or replace the superstitions of popular Hinduism by the superstitions of materialistic Science.

Our first necessity, if India is to survive and do her appointed work in the world, is that the youth of India should learn to think,—to think on all subjects, to think independently, fruitfully, going to the heart of things, not stopped by their surface, free of prejudgments, shearing sophism and prejudice asunder as with a sharp sword, smiting down obscurantism of all kinds as with the mace of Bhima....

Let us not, either, select at random, make a nameless hotchpotch and then triumphantly call it the assimilation of East and West. We must begin by accepting nothing on trust from any source whatsoever, by questioning everything and forming our own conclusions. We need not fear that we shall by that process cease to be Indians or fall into the danger of abandoning Hinduism. India can never cease to be India or Hinduism to be Hinduism, if we really think for ourselves. It is only if we allow Europe to think for us that India is in danger of becoming an ill-executed and foolish copy of Europe.... We must ... take our stand on that which is true and lasting. But in order to find out what in our conceptions is true and lasting, we must question all alike rigorously and impartially. The necessity of such a process not for India, but for all humanity has been recognised by leading European thinkers. It was what Carlyle meant when he spoke of swallowing all formulas. It was the process by which Goethe helped to reinvigorate European thinking. But ... Europe has for some time ceased to produce original thinkers, though it still produces original mechanicians.... China, Japan and the Mussulman states are sliding into a blind European imitativeness. In India alone there is self-contained, dormant, the energy and the invincible spiritual individuality which can yet arise and break her own and the world's fetters.[18]

*

Even causes hopelessly lost and deserving to be lost will find their defenders and unworthy altars do not lack incense.[19]

*

Reform is not an excellent thing in itself as many Europe-anised intellects imagine; neither is it always safe and good to stand unmoved in the ancient paths as the orthodox obsti-nately believe. Reform is sometimes the first step to the abyss, but immobility is the most perfect way to stagnate and to putrefy. Neither is moderation always the wisest counsel: the mean is not always golden. It is often an euphemism for purblindness, for a tepid indifference or for a cowardly inef-ficiency. Men call themselves moderates, conservatives or extremists and manage their conduct and opinions in accord-ance with a formula. We like to think by systems and parties and forget that truth is the only standard. Systems are merely convenient cases for keeping arranged knowledge, parties a useful machinery for combined action; but we make of them an excuse for avoiding the trouble of thought.

One is astonished at the position of the orthodox. They labour to deify everything that exists. Hindu society has cer-tain arrangements and habits which are merely customary. There is no proof that they existed in ancient times nor any reason why they should last into the future.... Neither anti-quity nor modernity can be the test of truth or the test of usefulness. All the Rishis do not belong to the past; the Avatars still come; revelation still continues.... To recreate Manu entire in modern society is to ask Ganges to flow back to the Himalayas. Manu is no doubt national, but so is the animal sacrifice and the burnt offering. Because a thing is national of the past, it need not follow that it must be national of the future. It is stupid not to recognise altered conditions.... To all things there is a date and a limit. All long-continued customs have been sovereignly useful in their time, even totemism and polyandry. We must not ignore the usefulness of the past, but we seek in preference a present and a future utility.

Custom and Law may then be altered. For each age its Shastra. But we cannot argue straight off that it must be altered, or even if alteration is necessary, that it must be

altered in a given direction. One is repelled by the ignorant
enthusiasm of social reformers. Their minds are usually a
strange jumble of ill-digested European notions. Very few of
them know anything about Europe, and even those who have
visited it know it badly. But they will not allow things or ideas
contrary to European notions to be anything but superstitious, barbarous, harmful and benighted, they will not suffer
what is praised and practised in Europe to be anything but
rational and enlightened....

Almost every point that the social reformers raise could be
settled one way or the other without effecting the permanent
good of society. It is pitiful to see men labouring the point of
marriage between subcastes and triumphing over an isolated
instance. Whether the spirit as well as the body of caste should
remain, is the modern question. Let Hindus remember that
caste as it stands is merely *jāt*, the trade guild sanctified but
no longer working, it is not the eternal religion, it is not *cātur-
varnya*. I do not care whether widows marry or remain single;
but it is of infinite importance to consider how woman shall
be legally and socially related to man, as his inferior, equal
or superior; for even the relation of superiority is no more
impossible in the future than it was in the far-distant past.
And the most important question of all is whether society
shall be competitive or cooperative, individualistic or communistic. That we should talk so little about these things
and be stormy over insignificant details, shows painfully the
impoverishment of the average Indian intellect. If these
greater things are decided, as they must be, the smaller will
arrange themselves....

Men have long been troubling themselves about social
reform and blameless orthodoxy, and orthodoxy has crumbled
without social reform being effected. But all the time God
has been going about India getting His work done in spite of
the talking. Unknown to men the social revolution prepares
itself, and it is not in the direction they think, for it embraces
the world, not India only. Whether we like it or not, He will

sweep out the refuse of the Indian past and the European present. But the broom is not always sufficient; sometimes He uses the sword in preference. It seems probable that it will be used, for the world does not mend itself quickly, and therefore it will have violently to be mended....

Men cry out dismally and lament that all is perishing. But if they trust in God's Love and Wisdom, not preferring to it their conservative and narrow notions, they would rather insist that all is being reborn.

So much depends on Time and God's immediate purpose that it is more important to seek out His purpose than to attach ourselves to our own nostrums. The Kāla Purusha, Zeitgeist and Death-Spirit, has risen to his dreadful work—*lokaksayakrt pravrddhah*, increasing to destroy a world [Gita, 11.32],—and who shall stay the terror and mightiness and irresistibility of Him? But He is not only destroying the world that was, He is creating the world that shall be; it is therefore more profitable for us to discover and help what He is building than to lament and hug in our arms what He is destroying.... Kali is the age for a destruction and rebirth, not for a desperate clinging to the old that can no longer be saved....

Has the time arrived for that destruction? We think that it has. Listen to the crash of those waters, more formidable than the noise of assault,—mark that slow, sullen, remorseless sapping,—watch pile after pile of our patched incoherent ramshackle structure corroding, creaking, shaking with the blows, breaking, sinking silently or with a splash, suddenly or little by little into the yeast of those billows. Has the time arrived for a new construction? We say it has. Mark the activity, eagerness and hurrying to and fro of mankind, the rapid prospecting, seeking, digging, founding,—see the Avatars and great *vibhūtis* coming, arising thickly, treading each close behind the other. Are not these the signs and do they not tell us that the great Avatar of all arrives to establish the first Satya Yuga of the Kali?...

Yes, a new harmony, but not the scrannel pipes of European

materialism, not an Occidental foundation upon half truths and whole falsehoods. When there is destruction, it is the form that perishes, not the spirit—for the world and its ways are forms of one Truth which appears in this material world in ever new bodies.... In India, the chosen land, [that Truth] is preserved; in the soul of India it sleeps expectant on that soul's awakening, the soul of India leonine, luminous, locked in the closed petals of the ancient lotus of love, strength and wisdom, not in her weak, soiled, transient and miserable externals. India alone can build the future of mankind.[20]

*

Ancient or pre-Buddhistic Hinduism sought Him both in the world and outside it; it took its stand on the strength and beauty and joy of the Veda, unlike modern or post-Buddhistic Hinduism which is oppressed with Buddha's sense of universal sorrow and Shankara's sense of universal illusion,— Shankara who was the better able to destroy Buddhism because he was himself half a Buddhist. Ancient Hinduism aimed socially at our fulfilment in God in life, modern Hinduism at the escape from life to God. The more modern ideal is fruitful of a noble and ascetic spirituality, but has a chilling and hostile effect on social soundness and development; social life under its shadow stagnates for want of belief and delight, *sraddhā* and *ānanda*. If we are to make our society perfect and the nation is to live again, then we must revert to the earlier and fuller truth.[21]

*
* *

**July 13, 1911**

*(From a letter to a friend.)*

Be very careful to follow my instructions in avoiding the old kind of politics. Spirituality is India's only politics, the fulfilment of the Sanatana Dharma its only Swaraj. I have no doubt we shall have to go through our Parliamentary period in order to get rid of the notion of Western democracy by seeing in practice how helpless it is to make nations blessed. India is passing really through the first stages of a sort of national Yoga. It was mastered in the inception by the inrush of divine force which came in 1905 and aroused it from its state of complete tamasic *ajñānam* [ignorance]. But, as happens also with individuals, all that was evil, all the wrong *samskāras* [imprints] and wrong emotions and mental and moral habits rose with it and misused the divine force. Hence all that orgy of political oratory, democratic fervour, meetings, processions, passive resistance, all ending in bombs, revolvers and Coercion laws.... God has struck it all down,—Moderatism, the bastard child of English Liberalism; Nationalism, the mixed progeny of Europe and Asia; Terrorism, the abortive offspring of Bakunin and Mazzini.... It is only when this foolishness is done with that truth will have a chance, the sattwic mind in India emerge and a really strong spiritual movement begin as a prelude to India's regeneration. No doubt, there will be plenty of trouble and error still to face, but we shall have a chance of putting our feet on the right path. In all I believe God to be guiding us, giving the necessary experiences, preparing the necessary conditions.[22]

*<br>* *

**1910-1914**

*(In the first years of his stay at Pondicherry, Sri
Aurobindo made a deep study of the Veda and, struck
by the light it threw on his own experiences, rediscov-
ered its lost meaning. A series of extracts from early
manuscripts on the Veda:)*

I seek not science, not religion, not Theosophy, but Veda—
the truth about Brahman, not only about His essentiality,
but about His manifestation, not a lamp on the way to the
forest, but a light and a guide to joy and action in the world,
the truth which is beyond opinion, the knowledge which all
thought strives after—*yasmin vijñāte sarvam vijñātam* [which
being known, all is known]. I believe that Veda to be the
foundation of the Sanatan Dharma; I believe it to be the concealed divinity within Hinduism,—but a veil has to be drawn
aside, a curtain has to be lifted. I believe it to be knowable
and discoverable. I believe the future of India and the world
to depend on its discovery and on its application, not to the
renunciation of life, but to life in the world and among men.[23]

\*

Men set up an authority and put it between themselves and
knowledge. The orthodox are indignant that a mere modern
should presume to differ from Shankara in interpreting the
Vedanta or from Sayana in interpreting the Veda. They forget
that Shankara and Sayana are themselves moderns, separated
from ourselves by some hundreds of years only, but the Vedas
are many thousands of years old. The commentator ought to
be studied, but instead we put him in place of the text. Good
commentaries are always helpful even when they are wrong,
but the best cannot be allowed to fetter inquiry. Sayana's
commentary on the Veda helps me by showing what a man of
great erudition some hundreds of years ago thought to be the

sense of the Scripture. But I cannot forget that even at the time of the Brahmanas* the meaning of the Veda had become dark to the men of that prehistoric age.... I find that Shankara had grasped much of Vedantic truth, but that much was dark to him. I am bound to admit what he realised; I am not bound to exclude what he failed to realise. *Āptavākyam*, authority, is one kind of proof; it is not the only kind: *pratyaksa* [direct knowledge] is more important.

The heterodox on the other hand swear by Max Müller and the Europeans.... The Europeans have seen in our Veda only the rude chants of an antique and primitive pastoral race sung in honour of the forces of Nature, and for many their opinion is conclusive of the significance of the *mantras*. All other interpretation is to them superstitious. But to me the ingenious guesses of foreign grammarians are of no more authority than the ingenious guesses of Sayana. It is irrelevant to me what Max Müller thinks of the Veda or what Sayana thinks of the Veda. I should prefer to know what the Veda has to say for itself and, if there is any light there on the unknown or on the infinite, to follow the ray till I come face to face with that which it illumines.[24]

*

Europe has formed certain views about the Veda and the Vedanta, and succeeded in imposing them on the Indian intellect.... When a hundred world-famous scholars cry out, "This is so," it is hard indeed for the average mind, and even minds above the average but inexpert in these special subjects not to acquiesce....

Nevertheless a time must come when the Indian mind will shake off the darkness that has fallen upon it, cease to think or hold opinions at second and third hand and reassert its right to judge and enquire in a perfect freedom into the

* The Brahmanas are the part of the Veda consisting of commentaries on the Mantras, instructions for rituals, myths and legends, etc.

meaning of its own Scriptures. When that day comes we shall, I think, discover that the imposing fabric of Vedic theory is based upon nothing more sound or true than a foundation of loosely massed conjectures. We shall question many established philological myths,—the legend, for instance, of an Aryan invasion of India from the north, the artificial and inimical distinction of Aryan and Dravidian which an erroneous philology has driven like a wedge into the unity of the homogenous Indo-Afghan race; the strange dogma of a "henotheistic" Vedic naturalism; the ingenious and brilliant extravagances of the modern sun and star myth weavers....[25]

\*

I will take this Puranic theory [of cycles of civilisation that preceded ours] as a working hypothesis and suppose at least that there was a great Vedic age of advanced civilisation broken afterwards by Time and circumstance and of which modern Hinduism presents us only some preserved, collected or redeveloped fragments.... We need not understand by an advanced civilisation a culture or a society at all resembling what our modern notions conceive to be the only model of a civilised society—the modern European; neither need or indeed can we suppose it to have been at all on the model of the modern Hindu. It is probable that this ancient culture had none of those material conveniences on which we vaunt ourselves,—but it may have had others of a higher, possibly even a more potent kind.

. . .

I believe the Vedas to hold a sense which neither mediaeval India nor modern Europe has grasped, but which was perfectly plain to the early Vedantic thinkers. Max Müller has understood one thing by the Vedic mantras, Sayana has understood another, Yaska had his own interpretations of their antique diction, but none of them understood what Yajñavalkya and Ajatashatrou understood.... It is because we do not understand the Vedas that three fourths of the Upanishads are a sealed book to us. Even of the little we think we can understand, much has been insecurely grasped and superficially comprehended.... For want of this key profound scholars have fumbled and for want of this guidance great thinkers gone astray,—Max Müller emitted his wonderful utterance about the "babblings of humanity's nonage," * Shankara left so much of his text unexplained or put it by as inferior truth for the ignorant, Vivekananda found himself compelled to admit his non-comprehension of the Vedantin's cosmological ideas and mention them doubtfully as curious speculations.... Only when we thoroughly know the great Vedic ideas in their totality shall we be able entirely to appreciate the profound harmonious and grandiose system of thought of our early forefathers.[26]

*

Religious movements and revolutions have come and gone or left their mark but after all and through all the Veda remains to us our Rock of the Ages, our eternal foundation.... The Upanishads, mighty as they are, only aspire to bring out, arrange philosophically in the language of later thinking and crown with the supreme name of Brahman the eternal knowledge enshrined in the Vedas. Yet for some two thousand years at least no Indian has really understood the Vedas.
. . .

I find in the Aryan and Dravidian tongues, the Aryan and

---

* "What can be more tedious than the Veda?" he also asked. Most other nineteenth-century European scholars agreed: "The verses of the Veda appear singularly prosaic," says Wilson, "and at any rate their chief value lies not in their fancy [sic] but in their facts, social and religious." Monier-Williams finds them "to abound more in puerile ideas than in striking thoughts and lofty conceptions." Griffith is struck by the "intolerable monotony of a great number of the hymns," whose language and style, according to Cowell, "is singularly artificial." The last, however, concedes that "far wider and deeper study is needed to pierce to the real meaning of these old hymns."

Dravidian races not separate and unconnected families but two branches of a single stock. The legend of the Aryan invasion and settlement in the Panjab in Vedic times is, to me, a philological myth.[27] *

*

The Veda was the beginning of our spiritual knowledge; the Veda will remain its end. These compositions of an unknown antiquity are as the many breasts of the eternal Mother of knowledge from which our succeeding ages have all been fed....

The recovery of the perfect truth of the Veda is therefore not

---

* And a most enduring one. Sri Aurobindo's luminously consistent and cogent exposition in *The Secret of the Veda* of its symbolic sense, which provided a detailed refutation of the "Aryan invasion theory," has been studiously ignored by most Western and Indian scholars, although of late some of the latter have begun to recognize the importance of Sri Aurobindo's discovery. Yet it is striking to note that this theory and its resulting contrived reconstruction of India's ancient history, still presented and taught—especially in India—as a solid certainty, not only finds no confirmation of any sort in archaeology (which on the contrary clearly refutes it—see next footnote), but is also in head-on contradiction with two mainstays of Indian tradition: 1. The one that regards the Ramayana and the Mahabharata as based on historical tradition *(itihāsa)*, considerably embellished, to be sure, but still with a kernel of historicity: we find depicted in these epics a highly developed civilization spanning several millennia, and a Great War waged around 3100 BC, both of which are incompatible with the semiprimitive cattle-worshipping Aryans' coming into India around 1500 BC; the Great War is therefore, at best, the glorification of a "local feud" between two Aryan tribes. 2. The more central tradition which holds the Veda to be a book of divine and eternal knowledge: most scholars find none in it, which is hardly surprising since they decide to force their reading of history, geography and ethnology into the Veda and a priori rule out any deeper, symbolic content to it (and consequently any significant spiritual experience the Vedic Rishis might have had); they are also compelled to date the Veda about 1000 BC, a ridiculously late date.

The result is the fallacy of a rigid break between Aryan and Dravidian races, languages, civilizations, even deities (Shiva is Dravidian, Vishnu is Aryan!). India, maimed in her spirit and her physical being, has also been maimed in her past. We await a broader, bolder and unblinkered scholarship, which will neither ignore the elements supplied by archaeology, nor close its eyes to what has been for millennia the source of India's spiritual life and strength.

merely a desideratum for our modern intellectual curiosity, but a practical necessity for the future of the human race. For I believe firmly that the secret concealed in the Veda, when entirely discovered, will be found to formulate perfectly that knowledge and practice of a divine life to which the march of humanity, after long wanderings in the satisfaction of the intellect and senses, must inevitably return.[28]

*

It is a superstition of modern thought that the march of knowledge has in all its parts progressed always in a line of forward progress deviating from it, no doubt, in certain periods of obscuration, but always returning and in the sum constituting everywhere an advance and nowhere a retrogression. Like all superstitions this belief is founded on bad and imperfect observation flowering into a logical fallacy.... The logical fallacy we land in as the goal of our bad observation is the erroneous conception that because we are more advanced than certain ancient peoples in our own especial lines of success, as the physical sciences, therefore necessarily we are also more advanced in other lines where we are still infants and have only recently begun to observe and experiment, as the science of psychology and the knowledge of our subjective existence and of mental forces.... While our forefathers believed that the more ancient might on the whole be trusted as more authoritative, because nearer to the gods, and the less ancient less authoritative because nearer to man's ultimate degeneracy, we [moderns] believe on the contrary that the more ancient is always on the whole more untrue because nearer to the unlettered and unenquiring savage, the more modern the more true because held as opinion by the lettered and instructed citizen of Paris or Berlin. Neither position can be accepted. Verification by experience and experiment is the only standard of truth, not antiquity, not modernity. Some of the ideas of the ancients or even of the savage now scouted by us may be lost truths or statements of

valid experience from which we have turned or become oblivi-
ous; many of the notions of the modern schoolmen will certainly in the future be scouted as erroneous and superstitious.[29]

*

The time-limit allowed for the growth of civilisation [by the
theory of a straight-line progression from a primitive age] is
still impossibly short.... We can no longer argue that no
ancient civilisations can have existed of which the traces have
entirely perished and that prehistoric means, necessarily,
savage and undeveloped.... Everything tends to show that
there must be the remains of other civilisations yet undiscov-
ered. We cannot have exhausted all that the earth contains.[30] *

*
* *

---

* Sri Aurobindo wrote this some eight years before the first archaeological
discoveries in 1921-22 of the Indus Valley or Harappan civilization (3500-1900
BC, now increasingly called Indus-Saraswati civilization). Since it had a priori
been decided that the "Vedic Aryans" entered India around 1500 BC, most
scholars felt compelled to conclude that this civilization was "pre-Aryan" and
pre-Vedic. Yet seals depicting deities seated in yogic postures, fire and
sacrificial altars, figures of the so-called Pasupati and the bull, worship of a
Mother goddess, recent indications of a marked affinity between the Indus
language and Vedic Sanskrit—all these are strongly suggestive of Vedic
culture, and indeed a number of archaeologists are veering to the view that
the Indus-Saraswati civilization was late or even post-Vedic. On the other
hand, they agree that no findings have been made east of the Indus which
could be traced to an Aryan people coming into India.
   More recent findings (in the 1980s) at Dwaraka and Bet-Dwaraka have put
one more spanner in the well-greased works of the Aryan invasion theory, as
they corroborate the submergence of Krishna's city, regarded till now as a
"myth" from the Mahabharata. Although the Dwaraka findings, carbon-
dated to about 1500 BC, do not as yet fit with the traditional date ascribed to
Krishna's time (let us however venture to suggest that further exploration
will reveal more ancient remains), even this "recent" date shows the absurdity of semiprimitive Aryan tribes invading India and instantly creating a
mighty urban civilization! Or else, if the Dwaraka ruins are a late development of the "pre-Aryan" Indus-Saraswati civilization, what becomes of its
association with "Aryan" Krishna, or at least (if Krishna is denied the honour
. . .

**1914-1915**

*(A few of Sri Aurobindo's
"Thoughts and Aphorisms")*

How much hatred and stupidity men succeed in packing up decorously and labelling "Religion"!

The quarrels of religious sects are like the disputing of pots, which shall be alone allowed to hold the immortalising nectar. Let them dispute, but the thing for us is to get at the nectar in whatever pot and attain immortality.

Break the moulds of the past, but keep safe its gains and its spirit, or else thou hast no future.

There are two for whom there is hope, the man who has felt God's touch and been drawn to it and the sceptical seeker and self-convinced atheist; but for the formularists of all the religions and the parrots of free thought, they are dead souls who follow a death that they call living.

---

of a physical existence) with the "Aryan" Mahabharata? Could this self-inflicted puzzle be the reason why S. R. Rao's rediscovery of ancient Dwaraka has not attracted the degree of attention which that of ancient Troy by Schliemann did?

Such has also been the fate of V. S. Wakankar's rediscovery in the 1980s of the bed of the Vedic river Saraswati, confirmed by satellite photography. This great river, now proved to have dried up before 2000 BC, is lavishly honoured in the Rig-Veda, supposedly composed by Aryan tribes a thousand years later! Moreover, some 700 Indus-Saraswati settlements have been found along its banks, further confirming the Vedic nature of this civilization. (An unbiased study of all available elements from archaeology, geography, mathematics, astronomy, etc., has now established that the Veda must have been composed between 7000 and 4000 BC.[31])

Whatever twists and turns Indian civilization may have followed, whatever migrations may have taken place to or from India, a sharp demarcation between pre- and post-Aryan India finds justification neither in the Scriptures nor in archaeology. It is safe to predict that future archaeological findings will further confirm the essential continuity of Indian civilization.

Thus said Ramakrishna and thus said Vivekananda. Yes, but let me know also the truths which the Avatar cast not forth into speech and the prophet has omitted from his teachings. There will always be more in God than the thought of man has ever conceived or the tongue of man has ever uttered.

*

The mediaeval ascetics hated women and thought they were created by God for the temptation of monks. One may be allowed to think more nobly both of God and of woman.

*

Fight, while thy hands are free, with thy hands and thy voice and thy brain and all manner of weapons. Art thou chained in the enemy's dungeons and have his gags silenced thee? Fight with thy silent all-besieging soul and thy wide-ranging will-power and when thou art dead, fight still with the world-encompassing force that went out from God within thee.

Thou thinkest the ascetic in his cave or on his mountain-top a stone and a do-nothing. What dost thou know? He may be filling the world with the mighty currents of his will and changing it by the pressure of his soul-state.

*

The existence of poverty is the proof of an unjust and ill-organised society, and our public charities are but the first tardy awakening in the conscience of a robber.

Selfishness kills the soul; destroy it. But take care that your altruism does not kill the souls of others.

*

Medical Science has been more a curse to mankind than a

blessing. It has broken the force of epidemics and unveiled a marvellous surgery; but, also, it has weakened the natural health of man and multiplied individual diseases; it has implanted fear and dependence in the mind and body; it has taught our health to repose not on natural soundness but a rickety and distasteful crutch compact from the mineral and vegetable kingdoms.

Machinery is necessary to modern humanity because of our incurable barbarism. If we must encase ourselves in a bewildering multitude of comforts and trappings, we must needs do without Art and its methods; for to dispense with simplicity and freedom is to dispense with beauty. The luxury of our ancestors was rich and even gorgeous, but never encumbered.

\*

The communistic principle of society is intrinsically as superior to the individualistic as is brotherhood to jealousy and mutual slaughter; but all the practical schemes of Socialism invented in Europe are a yoke, a tyranny and a prison.

If communism ever reestablishes itself successfully upon earth, it must be on a foundation of soul's brotherhood and the death of egoism. A forced association and a mechanical comradeship would end in a world-wide fiasco.

Democracy in Europe is the rule of the Cabinet minister, the corrupt deputy or the self-seeking capitalist masqued by the occasional sovereignty of a wavering populace; Socialism in Europe is likely to be the rule of the official and policeman masqued by the theoretic sovereignty of an abstract State. It is chimerical to enquire which is the better system; it would be difficult to decide which is the worse.

The gain of democracy is the security of the individual's life, liberty and goods from the caprices of the tyrant one or the selfish few; its evil is the decline of greatness in humanity.

This erring race of human beings dreams always of perfecting their environment by the machinery of government and society; but it is only by the perfection of the soul within that the outer environment can be perfected. What thou art within, that outside thee thou shalt enjoy; no machinery can rescue thee from the law of thy being.

Europe prides herself on her practical and scientific organisation and efficiency. I am waiting till her organisation is perfect; then a child shall destroy her.

*

So long as a cause has on its side one soul that is intangible in faith, it cannot perish.[32]

*
* *

**August 29, 1914**

*(From a letter to Motilal Roy, a revolutionary from Chandernagore who later attempted to create a commune based on Sri Aurobindo's ideals.)*

Gandhi's loyalism* is not a pattern for India which is not South Africa, and even Gandhi's loyalism is corrected by passive resistance. An abject tone of servility in politics is not "diplomacy" and is not good politics. It does not deceive or disarm the opponent; it does encourage nervelessness, fear and a cringing cunning in the subject people. What Gandhi has been attempting in South Africa is—to secure for Indians the position of kindly treated serfs,—as a stepping-stone to something better.... Our position is different and our aim is different, not to secure a few privileges, but to create a nation of men fit for independence and able to secure and keep it.

*
* *

**August, 1914**

In the fixed tradition of thousands of years [the Vedas] have been revered as the origin and standard of all that can be held as authoritative and true in Brahmana and Upanishad, in Tantra and Purana, in the doctrines of great philosophical schools and in the teachings of famous saints and sages. The name borne by them was Veda, the knowledge,—the received name for the highest spiritual truth of which the human mind is capable. But if we accept the current interpretations, whether Sayana's or the modern theory, the whole of this sublime and sacred reputation is a colossal fiction. The

---

* To the British Empire in South Africa during the Boer War (1899-1902) and the 1906 Zulu rebellion. When Sri Aurobindo wrote this letter, Gandhi was still in South Africa; he returned to India a few months later, in January, 1915.

hymns are, on the contrary, nothing more than the naive superstitious fancies of untaught and materialistic barbarians concerned only with the most external gains and enjoyments and ignorant of all but the most elementary moral notions or religious aspirations.[33]

\*\*\*

**September, 1914**

Western Philology has converted it [the word *ārya*] into a racial term, an unknown ethnological quantity on which different speculations fix different values.... [But] in the Veda the Aryan peoples are those who had accepted a particular type of self-culture, of inward and outward practice, of ideality, of aspiration....

Whoever seeks to climb from level to level up the hill of the divine, fearing nothing, deterred by no retardation or defeat, shrinking from no vastness because it is too vast for his intelligence, no height because it is too high for his spirit, no greatness because it is too great for his force and courage, he is the Aryan, the divine fighter and victor, the noble man.[34]

\*\*\*

**September, 1914 (?)**

*(From a letter to Motilal Roy.)*

You must understand that my mission is not to create Maths, ascetics and Sannyasis; but to call back the souls of the strong to the Lila of Krishna and Kāli.... Every ascetic movement since the time of Buddha has left India weaker and for a very obvious reason. Renunciation of life is one thing, to make life itself, national, individual, world-life greater and more divine is another. You cannot enforce one ideal on the country without weakening the other. You cannot take away the best souls from life and yet leave life stronger and greater. Renunciation of ego, acceptance of God in life is the Yoga I teach,—no other renunciation.

*<br>* *

**December, 1914**

Like the majority of educated Indians I had passively accepted without examination, before myself reading the Veda, the conclusions of European Scholarship both as to the religious and as to the historical and ethnical sense of the ancient hymns. In consequence, following again the ordinary line taken by modernised Hindu opinion, I regarded the Upanishads as the most ancient source of Indian thought and religion, the true Veda, the first Book of Knowledge. The Rigveda in the modern translations which were all I knew of this profound Scripture, represented for me an important document of our national history, but seemed of small value or importance for the history of thought or for a living spiritual experience....

It was my stay in Southern India which first seriously turned my thoughts to the Veda. Two observations that were forced on my mind gave a serious shock to my second-hand belief in the racial division between Northern Aryans and Southern Dravidians. The distinction had always rested for me on a supposed difference between the physical types of Aryan and Dravidian and a more definite incompatibility between the northern Sanskritic and the southern non-Sanskritic tongues. I knew indeed of the later theories which suppose that a single homogeneous race, Dravidian or Indo-Afghan, inhabits the Indian peninsula; but hitherto I had not attached much importance to these speculations. I could not, however, be long in Southern India without being impressed by the general recurrence of northern or "Aryan" type in the

Tamil race. Wherever I turned, I seemed to recognise with a startling distinctness, not only among the Brahmins but in all castes and classes, the old familiar faces, features, figures of my friends of Maharashtra, Gujerat, Hindustan, even, though this similarity was less widely spread, of my own province Bengal. The impression I received was as if an army of all the tribes of the North had descended on the South and submerged any previous populations that may have occupied it. A general impression of a Southern type survived, but it was impossible to fix it rigidly while studying the physiognomy of individuals. And in the end I could not but perceive that whatever admixtures might have taken place, whatever regional differences might have been evolved, there remains, behind all variations, a unity of physical as well as of cultural type* throughout India....

But what then of the sharp distinction between Aryan and Dravidian races created by the philologists? It disappears. If at all an Aryan invasion is admitted, we have either to suppose that it flooded India and determined the physical type of the people, with whatever modifications, or that it was the incursion of small bands of a less civilised race who melted away into the original population. We have then to suppose that entering a vast peninsula occupied by a civilised people, builders of great cities, extensive traders, not without mental and spiritual culture, they were yet able to impose on them their own language, religion, ideas and manners. Such a miracle would be just possible if the invaders possessed a very highly organised language, a greater force of creative mind and a more dynamic religious form and spirit.

And there was always the difference of language to support the theory of a meeting of races. But here also my preconceived ideas were disturbed and confounded. For on examining the

---

* I prefer not to use the term race, for race is a thing much more obscure and difficult to determine than is usually imagined. In dealing with it the trenchant distinctions current in the popular mind are wholly out of place. [Sri Aurobindo's footnote.]

vocables of the Tamil language,* in appearance so foreign to the Sanskritic form and character, I yet found myself continually guided by words or by families of words supposed to be pure Tamil in establishing new relations between Sanskrit and its distant sister, Latin, and occasionally, between the Greek and the Sanskrit. Sometimes the Tamil vocable not only suggested the connection, but proved the missing link in a family of connected words. And it was through this Dravidian language that I came first to perceive what seems to me now the true law, origins and, as it were, the embryology of the Aryan tongues. I was unable to pursue my examination far enough to establish any definite conclusion, but it certainly seems to me that the original connection between the Dravidian and Aryan tongues was far closer and more extensive than is usually supposed and the possibility suggests itself that they may even have been two divergent families derived from one lost primitive tongue. If so, the sole remaining evidence of an Aryan invasion of Dravidian India would be the indications to be found in the Vedic hymns.

It was, therefore, with a double interest that for the first time I took up the Veda in the original, though without any immediate intention of a close or serious study. It did not take long to see that the Vedic indications of a racial division between Aryans and Dasyus and the identification of the latter with the indigenous Indians were of a far flimsier character than I had supposed. But far more interesting to me was the discovery of a considerable body of profound psychological thought and experience lying neglected in these ancient hymns. And the importance of this element increased in my eyes when I found, first, that the mantras of the Veda illuminated with a clear and exact light psychological experiences of my own for which I had found no sufficient explanation either in European psychology or in the teachings of Yoga or of Vedanta, so far

---

* Sri Aurobindo studied Tamil for a few years with the help of Subramania Bharati, the well-known Tamil revolutionary and poet.

as I was acquainted with them, and, secondly, that they shed light on obscure passages and ideas of the Upanishads to which, previously, I could attach no exact meaning and gave at the same time a new sense to much in the Puranas.[35]

*\** \*

**1915 (?)**

*(Extracts from an interview given to a correspondent of* The Hindu*:)*

I am convinced and have long been convinced that a spiritual awakening, a reawakening to the true self of the nation is the most important condition of our national greatness.... India, if she chooses, can guide the world.

... I quite agree with you that our social fabric will have to be considerably altered before long.... Our past with all its faults and defects should be sacred to us; but the claims of our future with its immediate possibilities should be still more sacred.

*[The correspondent notes that Sri Aurobindo's "concluding words were spoken in a very solemn mood":]* It is more important that the thought of India should come out of the philosophical school and renew its contact with life, and the spiritual life of India issue out of the cave and the temple and, adapting itself to new forms, lay its hand upon the world. I believe also that humanity is about to enlarge its scope by new knowledge, new powers and capacities, which will create as great a revolution in human life as the physical science of the nineteenth century. Here, too, India holds in her past, a little rusted and put out of use, the key of humanity's future.

It is in these directions that I have been for some time impelled to turn my energies rather than to the petty political activities which are alone open to us at the present moment. This is the reason of my continued retirement and detachment from action. I believe in the necessity at such times and for such great objects of *tapasyā* in silence for self-training, for self-knowledge and storage of spiritual force. Our fore-fathers used that means, though in different forms. And it is the best means for becoming an efficient worker in the great days of the world.[36]

\*

*(From a letter to Motilal Roy.)*

It is regrettable that Bengal should be unable to find anything in the *Arya*,\* but not surprising. The intellect of Bengal has been so much fed on chemical tablets of thought and hot-spiced foods that anything strong and substantial is indigestible to it. Moreover people in India are accustomed only to second-hand thoughts,—the old familiar ideas of the six philosophies, Patanjali etc., etc. Any new presentation of life and thought and Yoga upsets their expectations and is unintelligible to them. The thought of the *Arya* demands close thinking from the reader; it does not spare him the trouble of thinking and understanding and the minds of the people have long been accustomed to have the trouble of thought spared them. They know how to indulge their minds, they have forgotten how to exercise them....

Soon after the *Arya* began, I got a letter from some graduates saying that what they wanted was "man-making." I have done my share of man-making and it is a thing which now anybody can do; Nature herself is looking after it all over the world, though more slowly in India than elsewhere. My business is now not man-making, but divine man-making. My present teaching is that the world is preparing for a new progress, a new evolution. Whatever race, whatever country seizes on the lines of that new evolution and fulfils it, will be the leader of humanity....

---

\* The monthly edited and published by Sri Aurobindo from 1914 to 1921.

India and especially Bengal have the best chance and the best right to create that race and become the leaders of the future,—to do in the right way what Germany thought of doing in the wrong way. But first they must learn to think, to cast away old ideas, and turn their faces resolutely to the future. But they cannot do this, if they merely copy European politics or go on eternally reproducing Buddhistic asceticism. I am afraid the Ramakrishna Mission with all its good intentions is only going to give us Shankaracharya and Buddhistic humanitarianism. But that is not the goal to which the world is moving.

*
* *

**January, 1915**

Charity and altruism are often essentially egoistic in their immediate motive. They are stirred by the discomfort of the sight of suffering to the nervous system or by the pleasurableness of others' appreciation of our kindliness or by the egoistic self-appreciation of our own benevolence or by the need of indulgence in sympathy. There are philanthropists who would be troubled if the poor were not always with us, for they would then have no field for their charity....

Nor is detailed sympathy and alleviation of particular sufferings the only help that can be given to men. To cut down branches of a man's tree of suffering is good, but they grow again; to aid him to remove its roots is a still more divine helpfulness.[37]

*
* *

**1915**

To be clear in one's own mind, entirely true and plain with one's self and with others, wholly honest with the conditions and materials of one's labour, is a rare gift in our crooked, complex and faltering humanity. It is the spirit of the Aryan worker and a sure secret of vigorous success. For always Nature recognizes a clear, honest and recognisable knock at her doors and gives the result with an answering scrupulosity and diligence.[38]

\* \*

*(On March 29, 1914, Sri Aurobindo met Mirra, a French lady who had come from France to see him. She stayed at Pondicherry for a year, went back to France, and in 1916 journeyed to Japan where she remained until her return to Pondicherry on April 24, 1920.*

*For thirty years she was going to work with Sri Aurobindo. We know her as "Mother."*

*Two passages from letters Sri Aurobindo wrote to Mother in France, while World War I was raging:)*

**May 6, 1915**

One needs to have a calm heart, a settled will, entire self-abnegation and the eyes constantly fixed on the beyond to live undiscouraged in times like these which are truly a period of universal decomposition.[39]

\*

*(From a letter of September 16, 1915.)*

It is a singular condition of the world, the very definition of chaos with the superficial form of the old world resting apparently intact on the surface. But a chaos of long disintegration or of some early new birth? It is the thing that is being fought out from day to day, but as yet without any approach to a decision.[40]

\* \*

**August, 1915**

The Vedic ritual, well-nigh obsolete, has lost its profound symbolic meaning; the pastoral, martial and rural images of the early Aryan poets sound remote, inappropriate, or, if natural and beautiful, yet void of the old deeper significance to the imagination of their descendants. Confronted with the stately hymns of the ancient dawn, we are conscious of a blank incomprehension. And we leave them as a prey to the ingenuity of the scholar who gropes for forced meanings amid obscurities and incongruities where the ancient bathed their souls in harmony and light.... The sense is dead and only the obscurity of a forgotten poetic form remains. Therefore when we read "Sarama by the path of the Truth discovers the herds", the mind is stopped and baffled by an unfamiliar language. It has to be translated to us ... into a plainer and less figured thought, "Intuition by the way of the Truth arrives at the hidden illuminations." * Lacking the clue, we wander into ingenuities about the Dawn and the Sun or even imagine in Sarama, the hound of heaven, a mythological personification of some prehistoric embassy to Dravidian nations for the recovery of plundered cattle![41]

*
* *

**August, 1915**

That stupendous effort [of Western materialism and civilisation] is over; it has not yet frankly declared its bankruptcy, but it is bankrupt. It is sinking in a cataclysm as gigantic and as unnatural as the attempt which gave it birth. On the other hand, the exaggerated spirituality of the Indian

---

* We cannot in these few extracts give a fair idea of the Vedic symbolism which Sri Aurobindo brought to light; the reader is invited to study his *Secret of the Veda*.

effort has also registered a bankruptcy; we have seen how high individuals can rise by it, but we have seen also how low a race can fall which in its eagerness to seek after God ignores His intention in humanity. Both the European and the Indian attempt were admirable, the Indian by its absolute spiritual sincerity, the European by its severe intellectual honesty and ardour for the truth; both have accomplished miracles; but in the end God and Nature have been too strong for the Titanism of the human spirit and for the Titanism of the human intellect.[42]

* *
*

**October, 1915**

*(From a book review in the* Arya.*)*

The book before us, Mr. O. C. Gangoly's *South Indian Bronzes*, must rank as one of the best of them all. Southern India, less ravaged than the North by the invader and the Vandal and profiting by the historic displacement of the centre of Indian culture southward, teems with artistic treasures.... But there are [in this book] some startlingly confident statements against which our critical sense protests. For instance, "it is *beyond doubt* that the two divisions of the country indicated by the Vindhya ranges were occupied by people essentially different in blood and temperament." Surely the important theories which hold the whole Indian race to be Dravidian in blood or, without assigning either an "Aryan" or "non-Aryan" origin, believe it to be homogeneous—omitting some islander types on the southern coast and the Mongoloid races of the Himalaya,—cannot be so lightly dismissed....

It distresses us to see Indian inquirers with their great opportunities simply following in the path of certain European scholars, accepting and adding to their unstable fantasies, their huge superstructures founded on weak and scattered evidence and their imaginative "history" of our prehistoric ages. There is better and sounder work to be done and Indians can do it admirably as Mr. Gangoly himself has shown in this book.[43]

* * *

### 1916

Either the Veda is what Sayana says it is, and then we have to leave it behind for ever as the document of a mythology and ritual which have no longer any living truth or force for thinking minds, or it is what the European scholars say it is, and then we have to put it away among the relics of the past as an antique record of semi-barbarous worship; or else it is indeed Veda, a book of divine knowledge, and then it becomes of supreme importance to us to know and to hear its message.
. . .

Dayananda's view is quite clear, its foundation inexpugnable. The Vedic hymns are chanted to the One Deity under many names, names which are used and even designed to express His qualities and powers. Was this conception of Dayananda's an arbitrary conceit fetched out of his own too ingenious imagination? Not at all; it is the explicit statement of the Veda itself: "One existent, sages"—not the ignorant, mind you, but the seers, the men of knowledge,—"speak of in many ways, as Indra, as Yama, as Matarishwan, as Agni" [*Rig-Veda*, I.164.46]. The Vedic Rishis ought surely to have known something about their own religion, more, let us hope, than Roth or Max Müller, and this is what they knew.

We are aware how modern scholars twist away from the evidence. This hymn, they say, was a late production, this loftier idea which it expresses with so clear a force rose up somehow in the later Aryan mind or was borrowed by those ignorant fire-worshippers, sun-worshippers, sky-worshippers from their cultured and philosophic Dravidian enemies. But throughout the Veda we have confirmatory hymns and expressions: Agni or Indra or another is expressly hymned as one with all the other gods. Agni contains all other divine powers within himself, the Maruts are described as all the gods, one deity is addressed by the names of others as well as his own, or, most commonly, he is given as Lord and King of the universe attributes only appropriate to the Supreme Deity. Ah, but that cannot mean, ought not to mean, must not mean, the worship of One; let us invent a new word, call it henotheism* and suppose that the Rishis did not really believe Indra or Agni to be the Supreme Deity but treated any god or every god as such for the nonce, perhaps that he might feel the more flattered and lend a more gracious ear for so hyperbolic a compliment! But why should not the foundation of Vedic thought be natural monotheism rather than this new-fangled monstrosity of henotheism? Well, because primitive barbarians could not possibly have risen to such high conceptions and, if you allow them to have so risen, you imperil our theory of the evolutionary stages of the human development and you destroy our whole idea about the sense of the Vedic hymns and their place in the history of mankind. Truth must hide herself, commonsense disappear from the field so that a theory may flourish! I ask, in this point, and it is *the* fundamental point, who deals most straightforwardly with the text, Dayananda or the Western scholars?

...

Dayananda goes farther; he affirms that the truths of modern physical science are discoverable in the hymns.... The ancient civilisations did possess secrets of science some of which modern knowledge has recovered, extended and made more rich and precise but others are even now not recovered. There is then nothing fantastic in Dayananda's idea that Veda contains truth of science as well as truth of religion. I will even add my own conviction that Veda contains other truths of a science the modern world does not at all

---

* A word coined by Max Müller.

possess, and in that case Dayananda has rather understated than overstated the depth and range of the Vedic wisdom.[44]

\* \*

**March, 1916**

Sanskrit ought still to have a future as a language of the learned and it will not be a good day for India when the ancient tongue ceases entirely to be written or spoken.\* But if it is to survive, it must get rid of the curse of the heavy pedantic style contracted by it in its decline with the lumbering impossible compounds and the overweight of hairsplitting erudition.[45]

\* \*

**May, 1916**

Human moderation is usually a wiseacre and a botcher; it sews a patch of new velvet on old fustian or of new fustian on old velvet and admires its deplorable handiwork. And its cautious advance means an accumulation of shams, fictions and dead conventions till the burden of falsehood becomes too great for life to bear and a violent revolution is necessary to deliver the soul of humanity out of the immobilising cerements of the past....

We have to face the future's offer of death as well as its offer of life, and it need not alarm us, for it is by constant death to our old names and forms that we shall live most vitally in greater and newer forms and names. Go on we must; for if we do not, Time itself will force us forward in spite of our fancied immobility. And this is the most pitiable and dangerous movement of all. For what can be more pitiable

---

\* Yet Sanskrit, the only language that was ever used over the whole of India and the one best expressive of her spirit and richness, is today on the way to extinction, its study discouraged in both North and South India.

than to be borne helplessly forward clinging to the old that disintegrates in spite of our efforts and shrieking frantically to the dead ghosts and dissolving fragments of the past to save us alive? And what can be more dangerous than to impose immobility on that which is in its nature mobile? This means an increasing and horrible rottenness; it means an attempt to persist on as a putrid and stinking corpse instead of a living and self-renewing energetic creature. The greatest spirits are therefore those who have no fear of the future, who accept its challenge and its wager; they have that sublime trust in the God or Power that guides the world....[46]

*

Help men, but do not pauperise them of their energy; lead and instruct men, but see that their initiative and originality remain intact; take others into thyself, but give them in return the full godhead of their nature. He who can do this is the leader and the *guru*.[47]

*
* *

**July, 1916**

In India the institution of slavery was practically absent and the woman had at first a freer and more dignified position than in Greece and Rome; but the slave was soon replaced by the proletariate, called in India the Shudra, and the increasing tendency to deny the highest benefits of the common life and culture to the Shudra and the woman brought down Indian society to the level of its Western congeners.[48]

*
* *

**August, 1916**

If we look at the beginnings of Indian society, the far-off Vedic age which we no longer understand, for we have lost

119

that mentality, we see that everything is symbolic.... Let us
take, for this example will serve us best, the Vedic institution
of fourfold order, *caturvarna*, miscalled the system of the
four castes,—for caste is a conventional, *varna* a symbolic
and typal institution.... This [symbolic significance of the
*caturvarna*] appears in the Purushasukta of the Veda where
the four orders are described as having sprung from the body
of the creative Deity, from his head, arms, thighs and feet. To
us this is merely a poetical image and its sense is that the
Brahmins were the men of knowledge, the Kshatriyas the
men of power, the Vaishyas the producers and support of
society, the Shudras its servants.... We read always our own
mentality into that of these ancient forefathers and it is
therefore that we can find in them nothing but imaginative
barbarians.... [But] to them this symbol of the Creator's
body was more than an image, it expressed a divine reality.
Human society was for them an attempt to express in life the
cosmic Purusha who has expressed himself otherwise in the
material and the supraphysical universe. Man and the cosmos
are both of them symbols and expressions of the same hidden
Reality.

...

[Later] in the evolution of caste, the outward supports of
the ethical fourfold order,—birth, economic function, religious ritual and sacrament, family custom,—each began to
exaggerate enormously its proportions and its importance in
the scheme. At first, birth does not seem to have been of the
first importance in the social order, for faculty and capacity
prevailed; but afterwards, as the type fixed itself, its maintenance by education and tradition became necessary and
education and tradition naturally fixed themselves in a hereditary groove. Thus the son of a Brahmin came always to be
looked upon conventionally as a Brahmin; birth and profession were together the double bond of the hereditary convention at the time when it was most firm and faithful to its own
character. This rigidity once established, the maintenance of

the ethical type passed from the first place to a secondary or even a quite tertiary importance.... Finally, even the economic basis began to disintegrate; birth, family custom and remnants, deformations, new accretions of meaningless or fanciful religious sign and ritual, the very scarecrow and caricature of the old profound symbolism, became the riveting links of the system of caste in the iron age of the old society. In the full economic period of caste the priest and the Pundit masquerade under the name of the Brahmin, the aristocrat and feudal baron under the name of the Kshatriya, the trader and money-getter under the name of the Vaishya, the half-fed labourer and economic serf under the name of the Shudra. When the economic basis also breaks down, then the unclean and diseased decrepitude of the old system has begun; it has become a name, a shell, a sham and must either be dissolved in the crucible of an individualist period of society or else fatally affect with weakness and falsehood the system of life that clings to it. That in visible fact is the last and present state of the caste system in India.[49]

\*
\* \*

**October, 1916**

[The Vedic Rishis] may not have yoked the lightning to their chariots, nor weighed sun and star, nor materialised all the destructive forces in Nature to aid them in massacre and domination, but they had measured and fathomed all the heavens and earths within us, they had cast their plummet into the inconscient and the subconscient and the superconscient; they had read the riddle of death and found the secret of immortality; they had sought for and discovered the One and known and worshipped Him in the glories of His light and purity and wisdom and power.[50]

* The whole Rig-veda reveals itself as a body of doctrine and practice, esoteric, occult, spiritual, such as might have been given by the mystics in any ancient country but which actually survives for us only in the Veda. It is there deliberately hidden by a veil, but the veil is not so thick as we first imagine; we have only to use our eyes and the veil vanishes; the body of the Word, the Truth stands out before us....

Our life is a battle between the powers of Light and Truth, the Gods who are the Immortals and the powers of Darkness. These are spoken of under various names as Vritra and Vritras, Vala and the Panis, the Dasyus and their kings. We have to call in the aid of the Gods to destroy the opposition of these powers of Darkness who conceal the Light** from us or rob us of it, who obstruct the flowing of the streams of Truth, *rtasya dhārāh* [Rig-Veda, V.12.2], the streams of Heaven and obstruct in every way the soul's ascent. We have to invoke the Gods by the inner sacrifice, and by the Word call them into us,—that is the specific power of the Mantra.... We give what we are and what we have in order that the riches of the divine Truth and Light may descend into our life and become the elements of our inner birth into the Truth.... Finally, as the summit of the teaching of the Vedic mystics comes the secret of the one Reality, *ekam sat* [I.164.46], or *tad ekam* [X.129.2], which became the central word of the Upanishads. The Gods, the powers of Light and Truth are powers and names of the One, each God is himself all the Gods or carries them in him: there is the one Truth, *tat satyam* [III.39.5], and one bliss to which we must rise.[51]

*<br>* *

---

* This text, although written in 1946 in the Foreword to *Hymns to the Mystic Fire*, has been included here in conclusion to the preceding series of extracts from Sri Aurobindo's writings on the Veda.
** Symbolized in the Veda by the cows or "shining herds."

## December, 1916

This is certain that there is not only no construction here without destruction, no harmony except by a poise of contending forces won out of many actual and potential discords, but also no continued existence of life except by a constant self-feeding and devouring of other life. Our very bodily life is a constant dying and being reborn, the body itself a beleaguered city attacked by assailing, protected by defending forces whose business is to devour each other.... It is good that we should be reminded of [this truth]; first, because to see it has for every strong soul a tonic effect which saves us from the flabbiness and relaxation encouraged by a too mellifluous philosophic, religious or ethical sentimentalism, that which loves to look upon Nature as love and life and beauty and good, but turns away from her grim mask of death, adoring God as Shiva but refusing to adore him as Rudra; secondly, because unless we have the honesty and courage to look existence straight in the face, we shall never arrive at any effective solution of its discords and oppositions. We must see first what life and the world are; afterwards, we can all the better set about finding the right way to transform them into what they should be. If this repellent aspect of existence holds in itself some secret of the final harmony, we shall by ignoring or belittling it miss that secret and all our efforts at a solution will fail by fault of our self-indulgent ignoring of the true elements of the problem....

War and destruction are not only a universal principle of our life here in its purely material aspects, but also of our mental and moral existence. It is self-evident that in the actual life of man intellectual, social, political, moral we can make no real step forward without a struggle, a battle between what exists and lives and what seeks to exist and live and between all that stands behind either. It is impossible, at least as men and things are, to advance, to grow, to fulfil and still to observe really and utterly that principle of harmlessness which is yet placed before us as the highest and best law of conduct. We will use only soul-force and never destroy by war or any even defensive employment of physical violence? Good, though until soul-force is effective, the Asuric force in men and nations tramples down, breaks, slaughters, burns, pollutes, as we see it doing today, but then at its ease and unhindered, and you have perhaps caused as much destruction of life by your abstinence as others by resort to violence.... Evil cannot perish without the destruction of much that lives by the evil....

It is not enough that our own hands should remain clean and our souls unstained for the law of strife and destruction to die out of the world; that which is its root must first disappear out of humanity. Much less will mere immobility and inertia unwilling to use or incapable of using any kind of resistance to evil, abrogate the law; inertia, Tamas, indeed, injures much more than can the rajasic principle of strife which at least creates more than it destroys. Therefore, so far as the problem of the individual's action goes, his abstention from strife and its inevitable concomitant destruction in their more gross and physical form may help his own moral being, but it leaves the Slayer of creatures unabolished.
...

It is only a few religions which have had the courage to say without any reserve, like the Indian, that this enigmatic World-Power is one Deity, one Trinity, to lift up the image of the Force that acts in the world in the figure not only of the beneficent Durga, but of the terrible Kali in her blood-stained dance of destruction and to say, "This too is the Mother; this also know to be God; this too, if thou hast the strength, adore." And it is significant that the religion which has had this unflinching honesty and tremendous courage, has succeeded in creating a profound and widespread spirituality such as no other can parallel. For truth is the foundation of real spirituality and courage is its soul.[52]

*
* *

**January, 1917**

The gospel of universal peace and goodwill among men —for without a universal and entire mutual goodwill there can be no real and abiding peace—has never succeeded for a moment in possessing itself of human life during the historic cycle of our progress, because morally, socially, spiritually the race was not prepared and the poise of Nature in its evolution would not admit of its being immediately prepared for any such transcendence. Even now we have not actually progressed beyond the feasibility of a system of accomodation between conflicting interests which may minimise the recurrence of the worst forms of strife. And towards this consummation the method, the approach which humanity has been forced by its own nature to adopt, is a monstrous mutual massacre unparalleled in history; a universal war, full of bitterness and irreconcilable hatred, is the straight way and the triumphant means modern man has found for the establishment of universal peace!.... A day may come, must surely come, we will say, when humanity will be ready spiritually, morally, socially for the reign of universal peace; meanwhile the aspect of battle and the nature and function of man as a fighter have to be accepted and accounted for by any practical philosophy and religion.[53]

*
* *

**February, 1917**

The Gita expressly says that Arjuna has thus lapsed into unheroic weakness [by his unwillingness to fight the enemies], because he is invaded by pity, *kripayāvistam*. Is this not then a divine weakness? Is not pity a divine emotion which should not thus be discouraged with [Krishna's] harsh rebuke? Or are we in face of a mere gospel of war and heroic action, a Nietzschean creed of power and high-browed strength, of

125

Hebraic or old Teutonic hardness which holds pity to be a weakness and thinks like the Norwegian hero who thanked God because He had given him a hard heart? But the teaching of the Gita springs from an Indian creed and to the Indian mind compassion has always figured as one of the largest elements of the divine nature....

It is this compassion in the Aryan fighter, the soul of his chivalry, which will not break the bruised reed, but helps and protects the weak and the oppressed and the wounded and the fallen. But it is also the divine compassion that smites down the strong tyrant and the confident oppressor, not in wrath and with hatred,—for these are not the high divine qualities, the wrath of God against the sinner, God's hatred of the wicked are the fables of half-enlightened creeds, as much a fable as the eternal torture of the Hells they have invented,—but, as the old Indian spirituality clearly saw, with as much love and compassion for the strong Titan erring by his strength and slain for his sins as for the sufferer and the oppressed who have to be saved from his violence and injustice.[54]

\*
\* \*

**March, 1917**

Civilisation can never be safe so long as, confining the cultured mentality to a small minority, it nourishes in its bosom a tremendous mass of ignorance, a multitude, a proletariate. Either knowledge must enlarge itself from above or be always in danger of submergence by the ignorant night from below. Still more must it be unsafe, if it allows enormous numbers of men to exist outside its pale uninformed by its light, full of the natural vigour of the barbarian, who may at any moment seize upon the physical weapons of the civilised without undergoing an intellectual transformation by their culture.... Knowledge must be aggressive, if it wishes to survive and perpetuate itself; to leave an extensive ignorance either below or around it, is to expose humanity to the perpetual danger of a barbaric relapse.

. . .

If Science has thus prepared us for an age of wider and deeper culture ... it has encouraged more or less indirectly both by its attitude to life and its discoveries another kind of barbarism,—for it can be called by no other name,—that of the industrial, the commercial, the economic age which is now progressing to its culmination and its close. This economic barbarism is essentially that of the vital man who mistakes the vital being* for the self and accepts its satisfaction as the first aim of life.... To the natural unredeemed economic man beauty is a thing otiose or a nuisance, art and poetry a frivolity or an ostentation and a means of advertisement. His idea of civilisation is comfort, his idea of morals social respectability, his idea of politics the encouragement of industry, the opening of markets, exploitation and trade following the flag, his idea of religion at best a pietistic formalism or the satisfaction of certain vitalistic emotions. He values education for its utility in fitting a man for success in a competitive or, it may be, a socialised industrial existence, science for the useful inventions and knowledge, the comforts, conveniences, machinery of production with which it arms him, its power for organisation, regulation, stimulus to production. The opulent plutocrat and the successful mammoth capitalist and organiser of industry are the supermen of the commercial age and the true, if often occult rulers of its society....

In a commercial age with its ideal, vulgar and barbarous, of success, vitalistic satisfaction, productiveness and possession the soul of man may linger a while for certain gains and experiences, but cannot permanently rest. If it persisted too

---

* The vital, in Sri Aurobindo's terminology, represents the region of consciousness between the physical and the mind, i.e. the region of emotions, feelings, passions, etc., which constitute the various expressions of the Life-Energy.

long, Life would become clogged and perish of its own plethora or burst in its straining to a gross expansion. Like the too massive Titan it will collapse by its own mass, *mole ruet sua*.[55]

\*
\* \*

**August, 1917**

*(A few "Thoughts and Glimpses.")*

Wherever thou seest a great end, be sure of a great beginning. Where a monstrous and painful destruction appals thy mind, console it with the certainty of a large and great creation. God is there not only in the still small voice, but in the fire and in the whirlwind.

The greater the destruction, the freer the chances of creation; but the destruction is often long, slow and oppressive, the creation tardy in its coming or interrupted in its triumph. The night returns again and again and the day lingers or seems even to have been a false dawning. Despair not therefore but watch and work. Those who hope violently, despair swiftly: neither hope nor fear, but be sure of God's purpose and thy will to accomplish.

Wherefore God hammers so fiercely at his world, tramples and kneads it like dough, casts it so often into the blood-bath and the red hell-heat of the furnace? Because humanity in the mass is still a hard, crude and vile ore which will not otherwise be smelted and shaped; as is his material, so is his method. Let it help to transmute itself into nobler and purer metal, his ways with it will be gentler and sweeter, much loftier and fairer its uses.

\*

Each religion has helped mankind. Paganism increased in man the light of beauty, the largeness and height of his life, his aim at a many-sided perfection; Christianity gave him some vision of divine love and charity; Buddhism has shown him a noble way to be wiser, gentler, purer; Judaism and Islam how to be religiously faithful in action and zealously devoted to God; Hinduism has opened to him the largest and profoundest spiritual possibilities. A great thing would be done if all these God-visions could embrace and cast themselves into each other; but intellectual dogma and cult-egoism stand in the way.

All religions have saved a number of souls, but none yet has been able to spiritualise mankind. For that there is needed not cult and creed, but a sustained and all-comprehending effort at spiritual self-evolution.

The changes we see in the world today are intellectual, moral, physical in their ideal and intention: the spiritual revolution waits for its hour and throws up meanwhile its waves here and there. Until it comes the sense of the others cannot be understood and till then all interpretations of present happening and forecast of man's future are vain things. For its nature, power, event are that which will determine the next cycle of our humanity.[56]

* * *

**December, 1917**

Each language is the sign and power of the soul of the people which naturally speaks it. Each develops therefore its own peculiar spirit, thought-temperament, way of dealing with life and knowledge and experience.... A nation, race or people which loses its language, cannot live its whole life or its real life. And this advantage to the national life is at the same time an advantage to the general life of the human race.[57]

* * *

**1918 (?)**

*("The Hour of God")*

There are moments when the Spirit moves among men and the breath of the Lord is abroad upon the waters of our being; there are others when it retires and men are left to act in the strength or the weakness of their own egoism. The first are periods when even a little effort produces great results and changes destiny; the second are spaces of time when much labour goes to the making of a little result. It is true that the latter may prepare the former, may be the little smoke of sacrifice going up to heaven which calls down the rain of God's bounty.

Unhappy is the man or the nation which, when the divine moment arrives, is found sleeping or unprepared to use it, because the lamp has not been kept trimmed for the welcome and the ears are sealed to the call. But thrice woe to them who are strong and ready, yet waste the force or misuse the moment; for them is irreparable loss or a great destruction.

In the hour of God cleanse thy soul of all self-deceit and hypocrisy and vain self-flattering that thou mayst look straight into thy spirit and hear that which summons it. All insincerity of nature, once thy defence against the eye of the Master and the light of the ideal, becomes now a gap in thy armour and invites the blow. Even if thou conquer for the moment, it is the worse for thee, for the blow shall come afterwards and cast thee down in the midst of thy triumph. But being pure cast aside all fear; for the hour is often terrible, a fire and a whirlwind and a tempest, a treading of the winepress of the wrath of God; but he who can stand up in it on the truth of his purpose is he who shall stand; even though he fall, he shall rise again; even though he seem to pass on the wings of the wind, he shall return. Nor let worldly prudence whisper too closely in thy ear; for it is the hour of the unexpected, the incalculable, the immeasurable. Mete not the power of the Breath by thy petty instruments, but trust and go forward.

But most keep thy soul clear, even if for a while, of the clamour of the ego. Then shall a fire march before thee in the night and the storm be thy helper and thy flag shall wave on the highest height of the greatness that was to be conquered.[58]

*
* *

## 1918

*(From a letter answering a request for Sri Aurobindo's opinion of a proposed law intended to facilitate marriages among Hindus of different castes.)*

I can only say that everything will have my full approval which helps to liberate and strengthen the life of the individual in the frame of a vigorous society and restore the freedom and energy which India had in her heroic times of greatness and expansion. Many of our present social forms were shaped, many of our customs originated, in a time of contraction and decline. They had their utility for self-defence and survival within narrow limits, but are a drag upon our progress in the present hour when we are called upon once again to enter upon a free and courageous self-adaptation and expansion. I believe in an aggressive and expanding, not in a narrowly defensive and self-contracting Hinduism....[59]

*

*(From an introduction to a book entitled
Speeches and Writings of Tilak.)*

The Congress movement was for a long time purely occidental in its mind, character and methods, confined to the English-educated few, founded on the political rights and interests of the people read in the light of English history and European ideals, but with no roots either in the past of the country or in the inner spirit of the nation.... To bring in the mass of the people, to found the greatness of the future on the greatness of the past, to infuse Indian politics with Indian religious fervour and spirituality are the indispensable conditions for a great and powerful political awakening in India. Others, writers, thinkers, spiritual leaders, had seen this truth. Mr. Tilak was the first to bring it into the actual field of practical politics.

...

There are always two classes of political mind: one is preoccupied with details for their own sake, revels in the petty points of the moment and puts away into the background the great principles and the great necessities, the other sees rather these first and always and details only in relation to them. The one type moves in a routine circle which may or may not have an issue; it cannot see the forest for the trees and it is only by an accident that it stumbles, if at all, on the way out. The other type takes a mountain-top view of the goal and all the directions and keeps that in its mental compass through all the deflections, retardations and tortuosities which the character of the intervening country may compel it to accept; but these it abridges as much as possible. The former class arrogate the name of statesman in their own day; it is to the latter that posterity concedes it and sees in them the true leaders of great movements. Mr. Tilak, like all men of pre-eminent political genius, belongs to this second and greater order of mind.[60]

\*
\* \*

**April, 1918**

*(Extracts from a message on national education
published in* New India *of April 8, 1918,
a journal edited by Annie Besant.)*

The greatest knowledge and the greatest riches man can
possess are [India's] by inheritance; she has that for which
all mankind is waiting.... But the full soul rich with the
inheritance of the past, the widening gains of the present,
and the large potentiality of the future, can come only by a
system of National Education. It cannot come by any extension
or imitation of the system of the existing universities with its
radically false principles, its vicious and mechanical methods,
its dead-alive routine tradition and its narrow and sightless
spirit. Only a new spirit and a new body born from the heart
of the Nation and full of the light and hope of its resurgence
can create it....

The new education will open careers which will be at once
ways of honourable sufficiency, dignity and affluence to the
individual, and paths of service to the country. For the men
who come out equipped in every way from its institutions
will be those who will give that impetus to the economic life
and effort of the country without which it cannot survive in
the press of the world, much less attain its high legitimate
position. Individual interest and National interest are the
same and call in the same direction.

. . .

Habituated individually always to the customary groove,
we prefer the safe and prescribed path, even when it leads
nowhere, to the great and effective way, and cannot see our
own interest because it presents itself in a new and untried
form. But this is a littleness of spirit which the Nation must
shake off that it may have the courage of its destiny....

This is an hour in which, for India as for all the world, its
future destiny and the turn of its steps for a century are being

powerfully decided, and for no ordinary century, but one which is itself a great turning-point, an immense turn-over in the inner and outer history of mankind. As we act now, so shall the reward of our Karma be meted out to us, and each call of this kind at such an hour is at once an opportunity, a choice, and a test offered to the spirit of our people.[61]

\*

It is found that civilisation has created many more problems than it can solve, has multiplied excessive needs and desires the satisfaction of which it has not sufficient vital force to sustain, has developed a jungle of claims and artificial instincts in the midst of which life loses its way and has no longer any sight of its aim. The more advanced minds begin to declare civilisation a failure and society begins to feel that they are right. But the remedy proposed is either a halt or even a retrogression, which means in the end more confusion, stagnation and decay, or a reversion to "Nature" which is impossible or can only come about by a cataclysm and disintegration of society; or even a cure is aimed at by carrying artificial remedies to their acme, by more and more Science, more and more mechanical devices, a more scientific organisation of life, which means that the engine shall replace life, the arbitrary logical reason substitute itself for complex Nature and man be saved by machinery. As well say that to carry a disease to its height is the best way to its cure....

The radical defect of all our systems is their deficient development of just that which society has most neglected, the spiritual element, the soul in man which is his true being.
...

The true and full spiritual aim in society will regard man not as a mind, a life and a body, but as a soul incarnated for a divine fulfilment upon earth, not only in heavens beyond, which after all it need not have left if it had no divine business here in the world of physical, vital and mental nature....

Therefore it will hold sacred all the different parts of man's life which correspond to the parts of his being, all his physical, vital dynamic, emotional, aesthetic, ethical, intellectual, psychic evolution, and see in them instruments for a growth towards a diviner living.[62]

*<br>* *

**May, 1918**

Man's road to spiritual supermanhood will be open when he declares boldly that all he has yet developed, including the intellect of which he is so rightly and yet so vainly proud, are now no longer sufficient for him, and that to uncase, discover, set free this greater Light within shall be henceforward his pervading preoccupation. Then will his philosophy, art, science, ethics, social existence, vital pursuits be no longer an exercise of mind and life, done for themselves, carried in a circle, but a means for the discovery of a greater Truth behind mind and life and for the bringing of its power into our human existence.[63]

*<br>* *

**June, 1918**

A spiritual age of mankind ... will not try to make man perfect by machinery or keep him straight by tying up all his limbs. It will not present to the member of the society his higher self in the person of the policeman, the official and the corporal, nor, let us say, in the form of a socialistic bureaucracy or a Labour Soviet. Its aim will be to diminish as soon and as far as possible the element of external compulsion in human life by awakening the inner divine compulsion of the Spirit within.[64]

*<br>* *

**July, 1918**

The ascent of man into heaven is not the key, but rather his ascent here into the spirit and the descent also of the Spirit into his normal humanity and the transformation of this earthly nature. For that and not some post mortem salvation is the real new birth for which humanity waits as the crowning movement of its long obscure and painful course.

Therefore the individuals who will most help the future of humanity in the new age will be those who will recognise a spiritual evolution as the destiny and therefore the great need of the human being.... They will especially not make the mistake of thinking that this change can be effected by machinery and outward institutions; they will know and never forget that it has to be lived out by each man inwardly or it can never be made a reality for the kind....

Failures must be originally numerous in everything great and difficult, but the time comes when the experience of past failures can be profitably used and the gate that so long resisted opens. In this as in all great human aspirations and endeavours, an *a priori* declaration of impossibility is a sign of ignorance and weakness, and the motto of the aspirant's endeavour must be the *solvitur ambulando** of the discoverer. For by the doing the difficulty will be solved. A true beginning has to be made; the rest is a work for Time in its sudden achievements or its long patient labour....

This endeavour will be a supreme and difficult labour even for the individual, but much more for the race. It may well be that, once started, it may not advance rapidly even to its first decisive stage; it may be that it will take long centuries of effort to come into some kind of permanent birth. But that is not altogether inevitable, for the principle of such changes in Nature seems to be a long obscure preparation followed

---

* The answer of Stephenson to those who argued by strict scientific logic that his engine on rails could not and should not move, "Your difficulty is solved by its moving." [Sri Aurobindo's footnote.]

by a swift gathering up and precipitation of the elements into the new birth, a rapid conversion, a transformation that in its luminous moment figures like a miracle.[65]

*
* *

**August, 1918**

When we look at the past of India, what strikes us ... is her stupendous vitality, her inexhaustible power of life and joy of life, her almost unimaginably prolific creativeness. For three thousand years at least,—it is indeed much longer,—she has been creating abundantly and incessantly, lavishly, with an inexhaustible many-sidedness, republics and kingdoms and empires, philosophies and cosmogonies and sciences and creeds and arts and poems and all kinds of monuments, palaces and temples and public works, communities and societies and religious orders, laws and codes and rituals, physical sciences, psychic sciences, systems of Yoga, systems of politics and administration, arts spiritual, arts worldly, trades, industries, fine crafts,—the list is endless and in each item there is almost a plethora of activity. She creates and creates and is not satisfied and is not tired; she will not have an end of it, seems hardly to need a space for rest, a time for inertia and lying fallow. She expands too outside her borders; her ships cross the ocean and the fine superfluity of her wealth brims over to Judea and Egypt and Rome; her colonies spread her arts and epics and creeds in the Archipelago; her traces are found in the sands of Mesopotamia; her religions conquer China and Japan and spread westward as far as Palestine and Alexandria, and the figures of the Upanishads and the sayings of the Buddhists are re-echoed on the lips of Christ. Everywhere, as on her soil, so in her works there is the teeming of a super-abundant energy of life....

Indeed without this opulent vitality and opulent intellectuality India could never have done so much as she did with her spiritual tendencies. It is a great error to suppose that spirituality flourishes best in an impoverished soil with the life half-killed and the intellect discouraged and intimidated. The spirituality that so flourishes is something morbid, hectic and exposed to perilous reactions. It is when the race has lived most richly and thought most profoundly that spirituality finds its heights and its depths and its constant and many-sided fruition.[66]

\*
\* \*

### September, 1918

... the shifty language of politics,—that strange language full of Maya and falsities of self-illusion and deliberate delusion of others, which almost immediately turns all true and vivid phrases into a jargon, so that men may fight in a cloud of words without any clear sense of the thing they are battling for....[67]

\*

The subjection of woman, the property of the man over the woman, was once an axiom of social life and has only in recent times been effectively challenged. So strong was or had become the instinct of this domination in the male animal man, that even religion and philosophy have had to sanction it.... This idea too is crumbling into the dust, though its remnants still cling to life by many strong tentacles of old legislation, continued instinct, persistence of traditional ideas; the fiat has gone out against it in the claim of woman to be regarded, she too, as a free individual being.[68]

\*
\* \*

### November, 1918

We are sometimes asked what on earth we mean by spirituality in art and poetry or in political and social life,—a confession

138

of ignorance strange enough in any Indian mouth at this stage of our national history.... We have here really an echo of the European idea, now of sufficiently long standing, that religion and spirituality on the one side and intellectual activity and practical life on the other are two entirely different things and have each to be pursued on its own entirely separate lines and in obedience to its own entirely separate principles....

Spirituality [does not mean] the moulding of the whole type of the national being to suit the limited dogmas, forms, tenets of a particular religion, as was often enough attempted by the old societies.... Spirituality is much wider than any particular religion.... True spirituality rejects no new light, no added means or materials of our human self-development. It means simply to keep our centre, our essential way of being, our inborn nature and assimilate to it all we receive, and evolve out of it all we do and create.... [India] can, if she will, give a new and decisive turn to the problems over which all mankind is labouring and stumbling, for the clue to their solutions is there in her ancient knowledge. Whether she will rise or not to the height of her opportunity in the renaissance which is coming upon her, is the question of her destiny.[69]

\*
\* \*

**December, 1918**

In the stupendous rush of change which is coming on the human world as a result of the present tornado of upheaval, ancient India's culture, attacked by European modernism, overpowered in the material field, betrayed by the indifference of her children, may perish for ever along with the soul of the nation that holds it in its keeping.... Each nation is a Shakti or power of the evolving spirit in humanity and lives by the principle which it embodies. India is the Bharata Shakti, the living energy of a great spiritual conception, and fidelity to it is the very principle of her existence....

To follow a law or principle involuntarily or ignorantly or contrary to the truth of one's consciousness is a falsehood and a self-destruction. To allow oneself to be killed, like the lamb attacked by the wolf, brings no growth, farthers no development, assures no spiritual merit. Concert or unity may come in good time, but it must be an underlying unity with a free differentiation, not a swallowing up of one by another or an incongruous and inharmonious mixture. Nor can it come before the world is ready for these greater things. To lay down one's arms in a state of war is to invite destruction and it can serve no compensating spiritual purpose....

India is indeed awaking and defending herself, but not sufficiently and not with the whole-heartedness, the clear sight and the firm resolution which can alone save her from the peril. Today it is close; let her choose,—for the choice is imperatively before her, to live or to perish.

. . .

A political Europeanisation would be followed by a social turn of the same kind and bring a cultural and spiritual death in its train.... Either India will be rationalised and industrialised out of all recognition and she will be no longer India or else she will be the leader in a new world-phase, aid by her example and cultural infiltration the new tendencies of the West and spiritualise the human race. That is the one radical and poignant question at issue. Will the spiritual motive which India represents prevail on Europe and create there new forms congenial to the West, or will European rationalism and commercialism put an end for ever to the Indian type of culture?[70]

*

The old world that is shaken outwardly in its bases and already crumbling in some of its parts, is the economical and materialistic civilisation which mankind has been forming for the last few centuries.... An era of revolutions has opened which is likely to complete the ruin and prepare the building of a new structure.

. . .

No paltering mechanisms which have the appearance but not the truth of freedom, will help us; the new structure, however imposing, will only become another prison and compel a fresh struggle for liberation. The one safety for man lies in learning to live from within outward, not depending on institutions and machinery to perfect him, but out of his growing inner perfection availing to shape a more perfect form and frame of life.... It is because there are plenty of signs that the old error continues and only a minority, leaders perhaps in light, but not yet in action, are striving to see more clearly, inwardly and truly, that we must expect as yet rather the last twilight which divides the dying from the unborn age than the real dawning. For a time, since the mind of man is not yet ready, the old spirit and method may yet be strong and seem for a short while to prosper; but the future lies with the men and nations who first see beyond both the glare and the dusk the gods of the morning and prepare themselves to be fit instruments of the Power that is pressing towards the light of a greater ideal.[71]

*
* *

**February, 1919**

Even in failure there is a preparation for success: our nights carry in them the secret of a greater dawn.
...

If the will in a race or civilisation is towards death, if it clings to the lassitude of decay and the laissez-faire of the moribund or even in strength insists blindly upon the propensities that lead to destruction or if it cherishes only the powers of dead Time and puts away from it the powers of the future, if it prefers life that was to life that will be, nothing, not even abundant strength and resources and intelligence, not even many calls to live and constantly offered opportunities will save it from an inevitable disintegration or collapse. But if there comes to it a strong faith in itself and a robust will to live, if it is open to the things that shall come, willing to seize on the future and what it offers and strong to compel it where it seems adverse, it can draw from adversity and defeat a force of invincible victory and rise from apparent helplessness and decay in a mighty flame of renovation to the light of a more splendid life. This is what Indian civilisation is now rearising to do as it has always done in the eternal strength of its spirit.[72]

*
* *

**April, 1919**

There is nothing in the most ascetic notes of the Indian mind like the black gloom of certain kinds of European pessimism, a city of dreadful night without joy here or hope beyond, and nothing like the sad and shrinking attitude before death and the dissolution of the body which pervades Western literature. The note of ascetic pessimism often found in Christianity is a distinctly Western note; for it is absent in Christ's teachings. The mediaeval religion with its cross, its salvation by suffering, its devil-ridden and flesh-

ridden world and the flames of eternal hell waiting for man
beyond the grave has a character of pain and terror alien
to the Indian mind, to which indeed religious terror is a
stranger....

Indian asceticism is not a mournful gospel of sorrow or a
painful mortification of the flesh in morbid penance, but a
noble effort towards a higher joy and an absolute possession
of the spirit.... Practised not by the comparatively few who
are called to it, but preached in its extreme form to all and
adopted by unfit thousands, its values may be debased, coun-
terfeits may abound and the vital force of the community
lose its elasticity and its forward spring. It would be idle to
pretend that such defects and untoward results have been
absent in India. I do not accept the ascetic ideal as the final
solution of the problem of human existence; but even its
exaggerations have a nobler spirit behind them than the
vitalistic exaggerations which are the opposite defect of
Western culture.[73]

\*
\* \*

**May, 1919**

[Hinduism] is in the first place a non-dogmatic inclusive
religion and would have taken even Islam and Christianity
into itself, if they had tolerated the process.[74]

\*

This world of our battle and labour is a fierce dangerous
destructive devouring world in which life exists precariously
and the soul and body of man move among enormous perils,
a world in which by every step forward, whether we will it or
no, something is crushed and broken, in which every breath
of life is a breath too of death. To put away the responsibility
for all that seems to us evil or terrible on the shoulders of a
semi-omnipotent Devil, or to put it aside as part of Nature,
making an unbridgeable opposition between world-nature

and God-Nature, as if Nature were independent of God, or to throw the responsibility on man and his sins, as if he had a preponderant voice in the making of this world or could create anything against the will of God, are clumsily comfortable devices in which the religious thought of India has never taken refuge. We have to look courageously in the face of the reality and see that it is God and none else who has made this world in his being and that so he has made it. We have to see that Nature devouring her children, Time eating up the lives of creatures, Death universal and ineluctable and the violence of the Rudra forces in man and Nature are also the supreme Godhead in one of his cosmic figures....

No real peace can be till the heart of man deserves peace; the law of Vishnu cannot prevail till the debt to Rudra is paid. To turn aside then and preach to a still unevolved mankind the law of love and oneness? Teachers of the law of love and oneness there must be, for by that way must come the ultimate salvation. But not till the Time-Spirit in man is ready, can the inner and ultimate prevail over the outer and immediate reality. Christ and Buddha have come and gone, but it is Rudra who still holds the world in the hollow of his hand. And meanwhile the fierce forward labour of mankind tormented and oppressed by the powers that are profiteers of egoistic force and their servants cries for the sword of the Hero of the struggle and the word of its prophet.[75]

\*
\* \*

**1919 (?)**

*(From a letter to Motilal Roy.)*

All difficulties can be conquered, but only on condition of fidelity to the Way that you have taken. There is no obligation on any one to take it,—it is a difficult and trying one, a way for heroes, not for weaklings,—but once taken, it must be followed, or you will not arrive.

144

...

Hunger-striking to force God or to force anybody or anything else is not the true spiritual means. I do not object to Mr. Gandhi or any one else following it for quite other than spiritual purposes, but here it is out of place; these things, I repeat, are foreign to the fundamental principle of our Yoga.

...

I myself have had for these fourteen years, and it is not yet finished, to bear all the possible typical difficulties, troubles, downfalls and backslidings that can rise in this great effort to change the whole normal human being.... We are the pioneers hewing our way through the jungle of the lower Prakriti. It will not do for us to be cowards and shirkers and refuse the burden, to clamour for everything to be made quick and easy for us. Above all things I demand from you endurance, firmness, heroism,—the true spiritual heroism. I want strong men. I do not want emotional children.

*<br>* *

**August, 1919**

The religious culture which now goes by the name of Hinduism ... gave itself no name, because it set itself no sectarian limits; it claimed no universal adhesion, asserted no sole infallible dogma, set up no single narrow path or gate of salvation; it was less a creed or cult than a continuously enlarging tradition of the Godward endeavour of the human spirit. An immense many-sided and many-staged provision for a spiritual self-building and self-finding, it had some right to speak of itself by the only name it knew, the eternal religion, *sanātana dharma*....

Now just here is the first baffling difficulty over which the European mind stumbles; for it finds itself unable to make out what Hindu religion is.... How can there be a religion which has no rigid dogmas demanding belief on pain of eternal damnation, no theological postulates, even no fixed theology, no credo, distinguishing it from antagonistic or rival religions? How can there be a religion which has no papal head, no governing ecclesiastic body, no church, chapel or congregational system, no binding religious form of any kind obligatory on all its adherents, no one administration and discipline? For the Hindu priests are mere ceremonial officiants without any ecclesiastical authority or disciplinary powers and the Pundits are mere interpreters of the Shastra, not the law-givers of the religion or its rulers. How again can Hinduism be called a religion when it admits all beliefs, allowing even a kind of high-reaching atheism and agnosticism and permits all possible spiritual experiences, all kinds of religious adventures?...

To the Indian mind the least important part of religion is its dogma; the religious spirit matters, not the theological credo....

Hinduism has always attached to [the organisation of the individual and collective life] a great importance; it has left out no part of life as a thing secular and foreign to the religious and spiritual life.... The people of India, even the "ignorant masses" have this distinction that they are by centuries of training nearer to the inner realities, are divided from them by a less thick veil of the universal ignorance and are more easily led back to a vital glimpse of God and Spirit, self and eternity than the mass of men or even the cultured elite anywhere else. Where else could the lofty, austere and difficult teaching of a Buddha have seized so rapidly on the popular mind? Where else could the songs of a Tukaram, a Ramprasad, a Kabir, the Sikh Gurus and the chants of the Tamil saints with their fervid devotion but also their profound spiritual thinking have found so speedy an echo and formed a popular religious literature? This strong permeation or close nearness of the spiritual turn, this readiness of the mind of a whole nation to turn to the highest realities is the sign and fruit of an agelong, a real and a still living and supremely spiritual culture.

...

The mentality of the West has long cherished the aggressive and quite illogical idea of a single religion for all mankind, a religion universal by the very force of its narrowness, one set of dogmas, one cult, one system of ceremonies, one array of prohibitions and injunctions, one ecclesiastical ordinance. That narrow absurdity prances about as the one true religion which all must accept on peril of persecution by men here and spiritual rejection or fierce eternal punishment by God in other worlds. This grotesque creation of human unreason, the parent of so much intolerance, cruelty, obscurantism and aggressive fanaticism, has never been able to take firm hold of the free and supple mind of India. Men everywhere have common human failings, and intolerance and narrowness especially in the matter of observances there has been and is in India.... But these things have never taken the proportions which they assumed in Europe. Intolerance has been confined for the most part to the minor forms of polemical attack or to social obstruction or ostracism; very seldom have they transgressed across the line to the major forms of barbaric persecution which draw a long, red and hideous stain across the religious history of Europe. There has played ever in India the saving perception of a higher and purer spiritual intelligence, which has had its effect on the mass mentality. Indian religion has always felt that since the minds, the temperaments, the intellectual affinities of men are unlimited in their variety, a perfect liberty of thought and of worship must be allowed to the individual in his approach to the Infinite.[76]

*
* *

**1920**

The will of a single hero can breathe courage into the hearts of a million cowards.[77]

*

No system indeed by its own force can bring about the change that humanity really needs; for that can only come by its growth into the firmly realised possibilities of its own higher nature, and this growth depends on an inner and not an outer change. But outer changes may at least prepare favourable conditions for that more real· amelioration,—or on the contrary they may lead to such conditions that the sword of Kalki* can alone purify the earth from the burden of an obstinately Asuric humanity. The choice lies with the race itself; for as it sows, so shall it reap the fruit of its Karma.[78]

*
* *

**January 5, 1920**

*(From a letter to Joseph Baptista, a co-worker of Tilak who had requested Sri Aurobindo to take up the editorship of a Nationalist English paper proposed to be brought out from Bombay. Sri Aurobindo explained his reasons for turning down this request, through which the Nationalists were hoping to give him an opportunity to return to politics.)*

---

* Kalki: the last Avatar, who comes riding a white winged horse, armed with a sword. He will come "like a burning comet."

Dear Baptista,

. . .

I do not at all look down on politics or political action or consider I have got above them. I have always laid a dominant stress and I now lay an entire stress on the spiritual life, but my idea of spirituality has nothing to do with ascetic withdrawal or contempt or disgust of secular things. There is to me nothing secular, all human activity is for me a thing to be included in a complete spiritual life, and the importance of politics at the present time is very great. But my line and intention of political activity would differ considerably from anything now current in the field. I entered into political action and continued it from 1903 to 1910 with one aim and one alone, to get into the mind of the people a settled will for freedom and the necessity of a struggle to achieve it in place of the futile ambling Congress methods till then in vogue. That is now done and the Amritsar Congress is the seal upon it....* What preoccupies me now is the question what [the country] is going to do with its self-determination, how will it use its freedom, on what lines is it going to determine its future?

You may ask why not come out and help, myself, so far as I can, in giving a lead? But my mind has a habit of running inconveniently ahead of the times,—some might say, out of time altogether into the world of the ideal. Your party, you say, is going to be a social democratic party. Now I believe in something which might be called social democracy, but not in any of the forms now current, and I am not altogether in love with the European kind, however great an improvement it may be on the past. I hold that India having a spirit of her own and a governing temperament proper to her own

---

* The 1919 Amritsar session declared Swaraj to be the aim of the Congress, as did the following 1920 Nagpur session; but this demand was soon eclipsed by the Khilafat movement (for the continuance of the Sultan of Turkey as the Caliph of the Mahomedan world), and returned to the fore only in 1929, at the Lahore session.

civilisation, should in politics as in everything else strike out her own original path and not stumble in the wake of Europe. But this is precisely what she will be obliged to do, if she has to start on the road in her present chaotic and unprepared condition of mind. No doubt people talk of India developing on her own lines, but nobody seems to have very clear or sufficient ideas as to what those lines are to be. In this matter I have formed ideals and certain definite ideas of my own, in which at present very few are likely to follow me,—since they are governed by an uncompromising spiritual idealism of an unconventional kind and would be unintelligible to many and an offence and stumbling-block to a great number.[79]

*
* *

**April, 1920**

> *(Barin Ghose, Sri Aurobindo's brother, was sentenced to death at the Alipore Bomb Case in 1909. On appeal his sentence was commuted to deportation for life to the Andamans; he was released early in 1920, after an amnesty. Soon afterwards, Barin wrote to Sri Aurobindo for guidance both from a political and a spiritual point of view. A few excerpts from Sri Aurobindo's long reply in Bengali.)*

What the Divine wants is for man to embody Him here, in the individual and in the collectivity—to realise **God in** life. The old system of yoga could not harmonise or **unify** Spirit and life; it dismissed the world as Maya or a transient play of God. The result has been a diminution of life-power and the decline of India. The Gita says, *utsīdeyur ime lokā na kuryām karma cedaham* ["These peoples would crumble to pieces if I did not do actions," 3.24]. Truly "these peoples" of India have gone to ruin. What kind of spiritual perfection is it if a few Sannyasins, Bairagis and Saddhus attain realisation

and liberation, if a few Bhaktas dance in a frenzy of love, god-intoxication and Ananda, and an entire race, devoid of life, devoid of intelligence, sinks to the depths of extreme tamas?
. . .
Why did I leave politics? Because our politics is not the genuine Indian article; it is a European import, just an imitation of European ways. But that too was needed. Both of us also engaged in politics of the European style; had we not done so, the country would not have risen, and we too would not have had the experience or obtained a full development....
But now the time has come to take hold of the substance instead of extending the shadow. We have to awaken the true soul of India and in its image fashion all works. For the last ten years I have been silently pouring my influence into this European political vessel, and there has been some result. I can continue to do this wherever necessary. But if I went out to do that work again, associating myself with the political leaders and working with them, it would be supporting an alien law of being and a false political life. People now want to spiritualise politics—Gandhi, for instance—but they can't get hold of the right way. What is Gandhi doing? Making a hodge-podge called *satyāgraha* out of *ahimsā paramo dharmah* [non-violence is the highest law], Jainism, *hartal*, passive resistance, etc.; bringing a sort of Indianised Tolstoyism into the country. The result—if there is any lasting result—will be a sort of Indianised Bolshevism. I have no objection to his work; let each one act according to his own inspiration. But that is not the real thing.
. . .
I believe that the main cause of India's weakness is not subjection, nor poverty, nor a lack of spirituality or Dharma, but a diminution of thought-power, the spread of ignorance in the motherland of Knowledge. Everywhere I see an inability or unwillingness to think—incapacity of thought or "thought-phobia". Whatever may have been in the mediaeval period, now this attitude is the sign of a great decline. The mediaeval

period was a night, a time of victory for the man of ignorance; the modern world is a time of victory for the man of knowledge. It is the one who can fathom and learn the truth of the world by thinking more, searching more, labouring more, who will gain more Shakti. Look at Europe, and you will see two things: a wide limitless sea of thought and the play of a huge and rapid, yet disciplined force. The whole Shakti of Europe lies there. It is by virtue of this Shakti that she has been able to swallow the world, like our Tapaswins of old, whose might held even the gods of the universe in awe, suspense and subjection. People say that Europe is rushing into the jaws of destruction. I do not think so. All these revolutions, all these upsettings are the initial stages of a new creation. Now look at India: a few solitary giants aside, everywhere there is your "simple man", that is your average man who will not think and cannot think, who has not the least Shakti but only a momentary excitement.... The difference lies there. But there is a fatal limitation to the power and thought of Europe. When she enters the field of spirituality, her thought-power stops working. There Europe sees everything as a riddle, nebulous metaphysics, yogic hallucination—"It rubs its eyes as in smoke and can see nothing clearly." Still, in Europe there is now a great striving to surmount even this limitation. Thanks to our forefathers, we have the spiritual sense, and whoever has this sense has within his reach such Knowledge, such Shakti that with one breath he could blow away like a blade of grass all the huge power of Europe. But to get that Shakti, Shakti is needed. We, however, are not worshippers of Shakti; we are worshippers of the easy way.... Our civilisation has become ossified, our Dharma a bigotry of externals, our spirituality a faint glimmer of light or a momentary wave of intoxication. So long as this state of things lasts, any permanent resurgence of India is impossible....

We have abandoned the sadhana of Shakti and so the Shakti has abandoned us. We practise the yoga of love, but where

there is no Knowledge or Shakti, love does not stay, narrowness and littleness come in. In a narrow and small mind, life
and heart, love finds no room. Where in Bengal is there love?
Nowhere else even in this division-ridden India is there so
much quarrelling, strained relations, jealousy, hatred and
factionalism as in Bengal. In the noble heroic age of the Aryan
people there was not so much shouting and gesticulating,
but the endeavour they set in motion lasted many centuries.
The Bengali's endeavour lasts for a day or two. You say what
is needed is emotional excitement, to fill the country with
enthusiasm. We did all that in the political field during the
Swadeshi period; but all we did now lies in the dust....
Therefore I no longer wish to make emotional excitement,
feeling and mental enthusiasm the base. I want to make a
vast and heroic equality the foundation of my yoga; in all the
activities of the being, of the *ādhār* [vessel] based on that
equality, I want a complete, firm and unshakable Shakti;
over that ocean of Shakti I want the vast radiation of the sun
of Knowledge and in that luminous vastness an established
ecstasy of infinite love and bliss and oneness. I do not want
tens of thousands of disciples; it will be enough if I can get
as instruments of God a hundred complete men free from
petty egoism. I have no faith in the customary trade of guru.
I do not want to be a guru. What I want is that a few, awakened at my touch or at that of another, will manifest from
within their sleeping divinity and realise the divine life. It is
such men who will raise this country.[80]

*<br>* *

**May, 1920**

*(From a letter to Motilal Roy.)*

The old politics in India persist in a chaos of parties and
programmes ... and in Bengal we have a rush of the commercial

and industrial spirit which follows the Western principle and, if it succeeds on these lines, is likely to create a very disastrous reproduction or imitation of the European situation with its corrupt capitalism and the Labour struggle and the war of classes.

...

People care nothing about the spiritual basis of life which is India's real mission and the only possible source of her greatness, or give to it only a slight, secondary or incidental value, a something that has to be stuck on as a sentiment or a bit of colouring matter. Our whole principle is different.

*
* *

**August, 1920**

Our call is to young India. It is the young who must be the builders of the new world,—not those who accept the competitive individualism, the capitalism or the materialistic communism of the West as India's future ideal, not those who are enslaved to old religious formulas and cannot believe in the acceptance and transformation of life by the spirit, but all who are free in mind and heart to accept a completer truth and labour for a greater ideal.... It is with a confident trust in the spirit that inspires us that we take our place among the standard-bearers of the new humanity that is struggling to be born amidst the chaos of a world in dissolution, and of the future India, the greater India of the rebirth that is to rejuvenate the mighty outworn body of the ancient Mother.[81]

*

We used the Mantra *Bande Mataram* with all our heart and soul, and so long as we used and lived it, relied upon its strength to overbear all difficulties, we prospered. But suddenly the faith and the courage failed us, the cry of the

Mantra began to sink and as it rang feebly, the strength began to fade out of the country. It was God, who made it fade out and falter, for it had done its work. A greater Mantra than *Bande Mataram* has to come. Bankim was not the ultimate seer of Indian awakening. He gave only the term of the initial and public worship, not the formula and the ritual of the inner secret *upāsanā* [worship]. For the greatest Mantras are those which are uttered within, and which the seer whispers or gives in dream or vision to his disciples. When the ultimate Mantra is practised even by two or three, then the closed Hand of God will begin to open; when the *upāsanā* is numerously followed the closed Hand will open absolutely.[82]

* *<br>*

**August 30, 1920**

*(From a letter to Dr. B. S. Munje, a Congress leader from Nagpur who asked Sri Aurobindo to return to British India to preside over the Nagpur session of the Congress a few months later.* Tilak had just passed away on August 1.)*

Dear Dr. Munje,

As I have already wired to you, I find myself unable to accept your offer of the Presidentship of the Nagpur Congress. There are reasons even within the political field itself which in any case would have stood in my way. In the first place I have never signed and would never care to sign as a personal declaration of faith the Congress creed, as my own is of a different character.... I am entirely in sympathy with all that is being done so far as its object is to secure liberty for

---

* Dr. Munje also visited Sri Aurobindo in October, 1920, and had long talks with him; he later became a leader of the Hindu Mahasabha.

India, but I should be unable to identify myself with the programme of any of the parties. The President of the Congress is really a mouthpiece of the Congress and to make from the presidential chair a purely personal pronouncement miles away from what the Congress is thinking and doing would be grotesquely out of place.

The central reason however is this that I am no longer first and foremost a politician, but have definitely commenced another kind of work with a spiritual basis, a work of spiritual, social, cultural and economic reconstruction of an almost revolutionary kind, and am even making or at least supervising a sort of practical or laboratory experiment in that sense which needs all the attention and energy that I can have to spare.

. . .

A gigantic movement of non-cooperation merely to get some Punjab officials punished or to set up again the Turkish Empire which is dead and gone, shocks my ideas both of proportion and of common sense.[83] *

\* \*
\*

**November, 1920**

*(From an article entitled*
*"A Preface on National Education.")*

The living spirit of the demand for national education no more requires a return to the astronomy and mathematics of Bhaskara or the forms of the system of Nalanda than the living spirit of Swadeshi a return from railway and motor traction to the ancient chariot and the bullock-cart.... It is the spirit, the living and vital issue that we have to do with, and there

---

* References to the officials responsible for the Jallianwala Bagh massacre, and to the Khilafat movement.

the question is not between modernism and antiquity, but between an imported civilisation and the greater possibilities of the Indian mind and nature, not between the present and the past, but between the present and the future. It is not a return to the fifth century but an initiation of the centuries to come, not a reversion but a break forward away from a present artificial falsity to her own greater innate potentialities that is demanded by the soul, by the Shakti of India.
. . .

A language, Sanskrit or another, should be acquired by whatever method is most natural, efficient and stimulating to the mind and we need not cling there to any past or present manner of teaching: but the vital question is how we are to learn and make use of Sanskrit and the indigenous languages so as to get to the heart and intimate sense of our own culture and establish a vivid continuity between the still living power of our past and the yet uncreated power of our future, and how we are to learn and use English or any other foreign tongue so as to know helpfully the life, ideas and culture of other countries and establish our right relations with the world around us. This is the aim and principle of a true national education, not, certainly, to ignore modern truth and knowledge, but to take our foundation on our own being, our own mind, our own spirit. . . .

The scientific, rationalistic, industrial, pseudo-democratic civilisation of the West is now in process of dissolution and it would be a lunatic absurdity for us at this moment to build blindly on that sinking foundation. When the most advanced minds of the occident are beginning to turn in this red evening of the West for the hope of a new and more spiritual civilisation to the genius of Asia, it would be strange if we could think of nothing better than to cast away our own self and potentialities and put our trust in the dissolving and moribund past of Europe.[84]

*
* *

**January, 1921**

India has never been nationally and politically one. India was for close on a thousand years swept by barbaric invasions and for almost another thousand years in servitude to successive foreign masters.... But in India at a very early time the spiritual and cultural unity was made complete and became the very stuff of the life of all this great surge of humanity between the Himalayas and the two seas.... Invasion and foreign rule, the Greek, the Parthian and the Hun, the robust vigour of Islam, the levelling steam-roller heaviness of the British occupation and the British system, the enormous pressure of the Occident have not been able to drive or crush the ancient soul out of the body her Vedic Rishis made for her.

...

India of the ages is not dead nor has she spoken her last creative word; she lives and has still something to do for herself and the human peoples. And that which must seek now to awake is not an anglicised oriental people, docile pupil of the West and doomed to repeat the cycle of the occident's success and failure, but still the ancient immemorable Shakti recovering her deepest self, lifting her head higher towards the supreme source of light and strength and turning to discover the complete meaning and a vaster form of her Dharma.[85]

*
* *

**November 18, 1922**

*(From a letter to Chittaranjan Das, the Nationalist leader who had defended Sri Aurobindo at the Alipore Bomb Case. C. R. Das came to Pondicherry to meet Sri Aurobindo in June, 1923; he passed away two years later, on June 16, 1925, his health broken by numerous imprisonments.)*

Dear Chitta,

. . .

I think you know my present idea and the attitude towards life and work to which it has brought me. I have become confirmed in a perception which I had always, less clearly and dynamically then, but which has now become more and more evident to me, that the true basis of work and life is the spiritual,—that is to say, a new consciousness to be developed only by Yoga. I see more and more manifestly that man can never get out of the futile circle the race is always treading until he has raised himself on to the new foundation. I believe also that it is the mission of India to make this great victory for the world. But what precisely was the nature of the dynamic power of this greater consciousness? What was the condition of its effective truth? How could it be brought down, mobilised, organised, turned upon life? How could our present instruments, intellect, mind, life, body be made true and perfect channels for this great transformation? This was the problem I have been trying to work out in my own experience and I have now a sure basis, a wide knowledge and some mastery of the secret....[86]

\*
\* \*

**December 1, 1922**

*(From a letter to Barin.)*

Dear Barin,

...

As you know, I do not believe that the Mahatma's principle [of non-cooperation] can be the true foundation or his programme the true means of bringing out the genuine freedom and greatness of India, her Swarajya and Samrajya.* On the other hand ... I hold that school [of Tilakite nationalism] to be out of date. My own policy, if I were in the field, would be radically different in principle and programme from both, however it might coincide in certain points. But the country is not yet ready to understand its principle or to execute its programme.

Because I know this very well, I am content to work still on the spiritual and psychic plane, preparing there the ideas and forces, which may afterwards at the right moment and under the right conditions precipitate themselves into the vital and material field....[87]

*\**
*\* \**

---

* I.e., her self-rule and perfect empire.

*Sri Aurobindo*
*around 1920*

# III

## 1923 — 1926

*(In these years, Sri Aurobindo used to have daily talks with a few disciples on a wide variety of subjects, from his yoga to the prevailing national or international situation. The following excerpts from these talks, noted down from memory by some of the disciples present, provide glimpses of Sri Aurobindo's views on India's political, social, cultural systems and her spiritual possibilities.)*

**April 9, 1923**

The ancients [in India] based their society on the structure of religion—I do not mean narrow religion but the highest law of our being. The whole social fabric was built up to fulfil that purpose. There was no talk in those days of individual liberty in the present sense of the term, but there was absolute communal liberty. Every community was completely free to develop its own religion—the law of its being. Even the selection of the line was a matter of free choice for the individual.... In ancient times each community had its own Dharma and within itself it was independent; every village, every city had its own organization quite free from all political control and within that every individual was free—free to change and take up another line for his development. But all this was not put into a definite political unit. There were, of course, attempts at that kind of expression of life but they were only partially successful. The whole community in India was a very big one and the community culture based on Dharma was not thrown into a kind of [political or national] organization which would resist external aggression.

*
* *

**April 18, 1923**

*(The short-lived display of Hindu-Muslim unity that followed the launch of the Khilafat agitation in 1920 soon gave way to renewed distrust and acrimony, which seized on issues such as Hindu processions playing music before mosques, killing of cows in public during Id, etc.; early in 1923 clashes broke out in Amritsar and Multan, now in Pakistan, and were going to recur with increasing frequency till the Partition—and after.)*

*(A disciple:) Did you read [Pandit Madan Mohan]
Malaviya's speech about the Multan riots and also
what C. Rajagopalachari has said?*

*(Sri Aurobindo:)* I am sorry they are making a fetish of this
Hindu-Muslim unity. It is no use ignoring facts; some day the
Hindus may have to fight the Muslims and they must prepare
for it. Hindu-Muslim unity should not mean the subjection of
the Hindus. Every time the mildness of the Hindu has given
way. The best solution would be to allow the Hindus to organize themselves and the Hindu-Muslim unity would take care of
itself, it would automatically solve the problem. Otherwise,
we are lulled into a false sense of satisfaction that we have
solved a difficult problem, when in fact we have only shelved
it.

*
* *

**July 23, 1923**

*(A disciple:) The Mahatma believes that non-violence
purifies the man who practises it.*

I believe Gandhi does not know what actually happens to
the man's nature when he takes to Satyagraha or non-violence.
He thinks that men get purified by it. But when men suffer, or
subject themselves to voluntary suffering, what happens is that
their vital being gets strengthened. These movements affect the
vital being only and not any other part. Now, when you cannot
oppose the force that oppresses, you say that you will suffer.
That suffering is vital and it gives strength. When the man who
has thus suffered gets power he becomes a worse oppressor....
    What one *can* do is to transform the spirit of violence. But
in this practice of Satyagraha it is not transformed. When you
insist on such a one-sided principle, what happens is that cant,
hypocrisy and dishonesty get in and there is no purification
at all. Purification can come by the transformation of the

impulse of violence, as I said. In that respect the old system in India was much better: the man who had the fighting spirit became the Kshatriya and then the fighting spirit was raised above the ordinary vital influence. The attempt was to spiritualize it. It succeeded in doing what passive resistance cannot and will not achieve. The Kshatriya was the man who would not allow any oppression, who would fight it out and he was the man who would not oppress anybody. That was the ideal....

*There is also the question of Hindu-Muslim unity which the non-violence school is trying to solve on the basis of their theory.*

You can live amicably with a religion whose principle is toleration. But how is it possible to live peacefully with a religion whose principle is "I will not tolerate you"? How are you going to have unity with these people? Certainly, Hindu-Muslim unity cannot be arrived at on the basis that the Muslims will go on converting Hindus while the Hindus shall not convert any Mahomedan. You can't build unity on such a basis. Perhaps the only way of making the Mahomedans harmless is to make them lose their fanatic faith in their religion....

*The Mahomedan religion was born under such circumstances that the followers never forgot the origin.*

That was the result of the passive resistance which they practised. They went on suffering till they got strong enough and, when they got power, they began to persecute others with a vengeance....

*Gandhi's position is that he does not care to remove violence from others; he wants to observe non-violence himself.*

That is one of the violences of the Satyagrahi that he does not care for the presssure which he brings on others. It is not non-violence—it is not "Ahimsa." True Ahimsa is a state of mind and does not consist in physical or external action or in avoidance of action. Any pressure in the inner being is a breach of Ahimsa.

For instance, when Gandhi fasted in the Ahmedabad mill-hands' strike to settle the question between mill-owners and workers, there was a kind of violence towards others. The mill-owners did not want to be responsible for his death and so they gave way, without, of course, being convinced of his position. It is a kind of violence on them. But as soon as they found the situation normal they reverted to their old ideas. The same thing happened in South Africa. He got some concessions there by passive resistance and when he came back to India it became worse than before.

*<br>* *

## September 12, 1923

The Mahomedan or Islamic culture hardly gave anything to the world which may be said to be of fundamental importance and typically its own; Islamic culture was mainly borrowed from others. Their mathematics and astronomy and other subjects were derived from India and Greece. It is true they gave some of these things a new turn, but they have not created much. Their philosophy and their religion are very simple and what they call Sufism is largely the result of gnostics who lived in Persia and it is the logical outcome of that school of thought largely touched by Vedanta.

I have, however, mentioned [in *The Foundations of Indian Culture*] that Islamic culture contributed the Indo-Saracenic architecture to Indian culture. I do not think it has done anything more in India of cultural value. It gave some new forms to art and poetry. Its political institutions were always semi-barbaric.

*<br>* *

**February 28, 1924**

... That is the history of every religion, sect or religious institution: it begins with religion and ends in commerce. Everywhere you find the same thing.

*

**March 7, 1924**

*(A disciple:) The Khilafat is steam-rollered.**

It is quite right that it should be gone; the new [Turkish] republic seems thorough and solid in its working....

*There are tendencies among the Muslims showing that fanaticism may disintegrate.*

That is not sufficient because it would not change their whole outlook. What is wanted is some new religious movement among the Mahomedans which would remodel their religion and change the stamp of their temperament. For instance, Bahaism in Persia which has given quite a different stamp to their temperament.**

*

---

* Mustapha Kemal, whose Nationalist forces deposed the Sultan in November, 1922, and who proclaimed Turkey a republic a year later, finally abolished the office of the Caliph early March, 1924. The Khilafat movement in India soon died a natural death, after however having succeeded in strengthening the Indian Muslims' sense of separateness.
** Unfortunately, this tendency was reversed and Bahaism proscribed in many Muslim countries; in Iran, Bahaism is still today the object of severe persecution and the official policy is "to block the Bahais' progress and development."

**June 2, 1924**

Gandhi is wonderstruck that his interpretation of the Gita is seriously questioned by a Shastri. I am rather wonderstruck at his claim to an infallible interpretation of the Gita.

*(A disciple:) He has criticized the Arya Samaj also.*

Yes, he has criticized Dayananda Saraswati who has, according to him, abolished image-worship and set up the idolatry of the Vedas. He forgets, I am afraid, that he is doing the same in economics by his Charkha and Khaddar, and, if one may add, by his idolatry of non-violence in religion and philosophy.

In that way every one has established idol-worship. He has criticized the Arya Samaj but why not criticize Mahomedanism? His statement is adulatory of the Koran and of Christianity which is idolatry of the Bible, Christ and the Cross. Man is hardly able to do without externals and only a few will go to the kernel.

*
* *

**August 17, 1924**

*(A few months earlier, Gandhi had sent his son Devadas to Pondicherry to see Sri Aurobindo.)*

He asked my views about non-violence. I told him, "Suppose there is an invasion of India by the Afghans, how are you going to meet it with non-violence?" That is all I remember. I do not think he put me any other question.

*
* *

**January 21, 1925**

If the Truth which the yoga [of Sri Aurobindo] wants to achieve is attained and if India accepts it, then it will give quite a new turn to Indian politics—different from European politics. It would be a profound change.

*
* *

**December 4, 1925**

So long as you need to be virtuous you have not attained the pure spiritual height where you have not to think whether the action is moral or not. People hastily conclude that when you ask them to rise above morality, you are asking them to sink below good and evil. That is not at all the case.... By morality you become more human, but you do not go beyond humanity. Morality has done much good to man, maybe; it has also done much harm.

*(A disciple:) But people always confuse morality with spirituality.*

Like the Christians to whom there is no difference between morality and spirituality. For instance, take this fast now announced [by Gandhi]. It is a Christian idea of atonement for sin. All those other reasons which are given make it rather ridiculous.

Indian culture knew the value of morality, and also its limitations. The Upanishads and the Gita are loud with and full of the idea of going beyond morality.

*
* *

**April 7, 1926**

It is the European idea that makes you think that the parliamentary form or constitution is the best. [In ancient India] we had great communal liberty and the communities were the centre of power and of national life. The king could not infringe the right of the commune.... If these rights were interfered with the people at once made themselves felt. That was the form which the genius of the race had evolved....

I don't understand why everything should be centralized as in the parliamentary constitution. We must have different, numerous centres of culture and power, full of national life spread all over the country and they must have political freedom to develop themselves.

*(A disciple:) Village organization can also help in the creation of such centres.*

Yes. But it is not by lectures and sermonizing to the village people, as we are trying to do now.... If you want to work in the village, you must take to a natural profession, go and settle down among the village people and be one of them. When they see that you are a practical man they will begin to trust you. If you go there and work hard for ten or fifteen years you will gain your status and you will be able to do something because they will be prepared to listen to you.

The parliamentary form would be hardly suitable for our people. Of course, it is not necessary that you should have today the same old forms [as in ancient India]. But you can take the line of evolution and follow the bent of the genius of the race.

\*  
\* \*

**May 18, 1926**

Life has no "isms" in it, Supermind* also has no "isms". It is the mind that introduces all "isms" and creates confusion. That is the difference between a man who lives and a thinker who can't: a leader who thinks too much and is busy with ideas, trying all the time to fit the realities of life to his ideas, hardly succeeds, while the leader who is destined to succeed does not bother his head about ideas. He sees the forces at work and knows by intuition those that make for success. He also knows the right combination of forces and the right moment when he should act....

Look at Indian politicians: all ideas, ideas—they are busy with ideas. Take the Hindu-Muslim problem: I don't know why our politicians accepted Gandhi's Khilafat agitation.** With the mentality of the ordinary Mahomedan it was bound to produce the reaction it has produced: you fed the force, it gathered power and began to make demands which the Hindu mentality had to rise up and reject. That does not require Supermind to find out, it requires common sense. Then, the Mahomedan reality and the Hindu reality began to break heads at Calcutta.*** The leaders are busy trying to square the realities with their mental ideas instead of facing them straight....

At one time it was thought that the mind could grasp the whole Truth and solve all the problems that face humanity.

---

* Sri Aurobindo called "Supermind" or "Supramental" the region of full Truth-Consciousness which will be the normal state of consciousness of the next stage of evolution, just as the mind is the normal consciousness of our human stage.

** From the outset Gandhi made it clear that the Khilafat question was in his view more important and urgent than that of Swaraj. He wrote: "To the Musalmans, Swaraj means, as it must, India's ability to deal effectively with the Khilafat question.... It is impossible not to sympathise with this attitude.... I would gladly ask for postponement of Swaraj activity if thereby we could advance the interest of the Khilafat."[88]

*** A reference to serious riots in Calcutta the previous month.

The mind had its full play and we find that it is not able to solve the problems. Now, we find that it is possible to go beyond mind and there is the Supermind which is the organization of the Infinite Consciousness. There you find the truth of all that is in mind and life.

For instance, you find that Democracy, Socialism and Communism have each some truth behind it, but it is not the whole Truth. What you have to do is to find out the forces that are at work and understand what it is of which all these mental ideas and "isms" are a mere indication. You have to know the mistakes which people commit in dealing with the truth of these forces and the truth that is behind the mistakes also. I am, at present, speaking against democracy; that does not mean that there is no truth behind it. I know the truth [behind democracy], but I speak against democracy because that mentality is at present against the Truth that is trying to come down.

*<br>* *

**June 1, 1926**

> *(A disciple:) These newspapers print anything they like. Can they print the talk that takes place in one's house?*

If you expect manners from modern newspapers you will be sorely disappointed in these democratic days. It is one of the blessings of modern democracy! If you were in America and did not give any interview, even then they would invent one! The press is a public institution; formerly, it was something dignified, but now the newspapers are the correct measure of the futility of human life.... It is the same with all other modern things—the press, the theatre, the radio; they drag down everything to the level of the crowd.... They succeed only if they can pamper the common man's tastes....

It is the same old question of the mass being pulled up by

something higher. But, as it always happens, instead of being pulled up it is the mass that pulls everything down to its level....

*Are things worse or becoming better?*

To me the condition of Europe, after the war especially, seems almost to be the same as that at the break-up and disintegration of the Roman Empire. There is the same tendency to plunge the world into barbarism again.

*<p style="text-align:center">* *</p>*

**June 22, 1926**

*(A disciple:) Are Indians more spiritual than other people?*

No, it is not so. No nation is entirely spiritual. Indians are not more spiritual than other people. But behind the Indian race there lives the past spiritual influence.

*Some prominent national workers in India seem to me to be incarnations of some European force here.*

They may not be incarnations, but they may be strongly influenced by European thought. For instance, Gandhi is a European—truly, a Russian Christian in an Indian body. And there are some Indians in European bodies!

*Gandhi a European!*

Yes. When the Europeans say that he is more Christian than many Christians (some even say that he is "Christ of the modern times") they are perfectly right. All his preaching is derived from Christianity, and though the garb is Indian the essential spirit is Christian. He may not be Christ, but at any rate he comes in continuation of the same impulsion. He is largely influenced by Tolstoy, the Bible, and has a strong Jain tinge in his teachings; at any rate more than by the Indian scriptures—the Upanishads or the Gita which he interprets in the light of his own ideas.

*Many educated Indians consider him a spiritual man.*

Yes, because the Europeans call him spiritual. But what he preaches is not Indian spirituality but something derived from Russian Christianity, non-violence, suffering, etc....

The Russians are a queer mixture of strength and weakness. They have got a passion in their intellect, say, a passionate intellect. They have a distracted and restless emotional being, but there is something behind it which is very fine and psychic, though their soul is not very healthy. And therefore I am not right in saying that Gandhi is a Russian Christian, because he is so very dry. He has got the intellectual passion and a great moral will-force, but he is more dry than the Russians. The gospel of suffering that he is preaching has its root in Russia as nowhere else in Europe—other Christian nations don't believe in it. At the most they have it in the mind, but the Russians have got it in their very blood. They commit a mistake in preaching the gospel of suffering, but we also commit in India a mistake in preaching the idea of *vairāgya* [disgust with the world].

*
* *

**June 23, 1926**

When Gandhi's movement was started, I said that this movement would lead either to a fiasco or to a great confusion. And I see no reason to change my opinion. Only I would like to add that it has led to both.

*
* *

**June 29, 1926**

In India we had nothing of the mental ideal in politics. We had a spontaneous and a free growth of communities developing on their own lines. It was not so much a mental idea as an inner impulse or feeling, to express life in a particular form. Each such communal form of life—the village, the town, etc., which formed the unit of national life, was left free in its own internal management. The central authority never interfered with it.

There was not the idea of "interest" in India as in Europe, i.e., each community was not fighting for its own interest; but there was the idea of Dharma, the function which the individual and the community has to fulfil in the larger national life. There were caste organizations not based upon a religio-social basis as we find nowadays; they were more or less guilds, groups organized for a communal life. There were also religious communities like the Buddhists, the Jains, etc. Each followed its own law—Swadharma—unhampered by the State. The State recognized the necessity of allowing such various forms of life to develop freely in order to give to the national spirit a richer expression.

Then over the two there was the central authority, whose function was not so much to legislate as to harmonize and see that everything was going on all right. It was generally administered by a Raja; in cases it was also an elected head of the clan, as in the instance of Gautama Buddha's father. Each ruled over either a small State or a group of small States or republics. The king was not a law-maker and he was not at the head to put his hand over all organizations and keep them down. If he interfered with them he was deposed because each of these organizations had its own laws which had been established for long ages.

The machinery of the State also was not so mechanical as in the West—it was plastic and elastic.

This organization we find in history perfected in the reign of Chandragupta and the Maurya dynasty. The period preceding this must have been a period of great political development in India. Every department of national life, we can see, was in the charge of a board or a committee with a minister at the head, and each board looked after what we now would call its own department and was left free from undue interference of the central authority. The change of kings left these boards untouched and unaffected in their work. An organization similar to that was found in every town and village and it was this organization that was taken up by the Mahomedans when they came to India. It is that which the English also have taken up. The idea of the King as the absolute monarch was never an Indian idea. It was brought from Central Asia by the Mahomedans.

The English in accepting this system have disfigured it considerably. They have found ways to put their hand on and grasp all the old organizations, using them merely as channels to establish more thoroughly the authority of the central power. They discouraged every free organization and every attempt at the manifestation of the free life of the community. Now attempts are being made to have the cooperative societies in villages, there is an effort at reviving the Panchayats. But these organizations cannot be revived once they have been crushed; and even if they revived they would not be the same.

If the old organization had lasted it would have been a successful rival of the modern form of government.

*(A disciple:) Is it possible to come back to old forms in modern times?*

You need not come back to the old forms, but you *can* retain the spirit which might create its own new forms....

It has been a special feature of India that she has to contain in her life all the most diverse elements and assimilate them. This renders her problem most intricate.

*If it is India's destiny to assimilate all the conflicting elements, is it possible to assimilate the Mahomedan element also?*

Why not? India has assimilated elements from the Greeks, the Persians and other nations. But she assimilates only when her central truth is recognized by the other party, and even while assimilating she does it in such a way that the elements absorbed are no longer recognizable as foreign but become part of herself. For instance, we took from the Greek architecture, from the Persian painting, etc.

The assimilation of the Mahomedan culture also was done in the mind to a great extent and it would have perhaps gone further. But in order that the process may be complete it is necessary that a change in the Mahomedan mentality should come. The conflict is in the outer life and unless the Mahomedans learn tolerance I do not think the assimilation is possible.

The Hindu is ready to tolerate. He is open to new ideas and his culture has got a wonderful capacity for assimilation, but always provided that India's central truth is recognized.

*Did India have the national idea in the modern sense?*

The "nation idea" India never had. By that I mean the political idea of the nation. It is a modern growth. But we *had* in India the cultural and spiritual idea of the nation....

Present-day Indians have got nothing to boast of from their past. Indian culture today is in the most abject condition, like the fort of Gingee—one pillar standing here, another ceiling there and some hall out of recognition somewhere!

\* \*

**July 1, 1926**

*(A disciple:) Didn't the non-cooperation movement give life to the country?*

Do you call that life? It was based on a falsehood. How could you expect it to create anything? Swaraj was sought to be established by spinning—could anything come from such a false ideal? Some life was given to the country during the Swadeshi days in Bengal. You ought to have seen what Bengal was before the Swadeshi movement to understand what it accomplished. At that time we gave forms and ideals which have since degenerated. Those forms have now been taken up and distorted. Mahatma Gandhi has a sort of force—by exerting it he advances to a certain extent but in reaction he goes back much farther....

The Satyagraha movement is only meant for Mahatma Gandhi and a few men like him—it ought not to be thrust upon a whole people.

People talk of village organization—let them first bring life to the villages and they will organize themselves.

. . .

In India the students generally have great capacities but the system of education represses and destroys these capacities. Look at the method of the classroom—the students must sit there for so many hours and pore over their books: all this is very injurious. What is needed is an atmosphere—a pervasive atmosphere of learning. The students should imbibe that, find out their own aptitudes and develop along those lines.... Under the proper system of education both the needs —the need of the individual and the need of the nation—can be reconciled.... That is the future education of the race if it is to make any real progress.

*
* *

**July 26, 1926**

Generally woman can be said to be more efficient on the physical plane, because she follows her intuitions. She is more able to arrange matter generally, goes straight to the thing to be done, while man wanders forth into ideas and mental constructions. It can be seen in politics; women would succeed better. Man is able to put more mental power, while the woman acts more psychically. Man is more intellectual and woman more intuitive. She is also very active on the vital plane.

*(A disciple:) But while woman has often been the source of inspiration to man, she has not produced any great creative work.*

Because she was not given any opportunity by social bondages. Whenever women have been given opportunity they have shown their capacity.... We have to wait a few generations in order to see them at work.

*
* *

**August 1, 1926**

The attempt to placate the Mahomedans was a false diplomacy. Instead of trying to achieve Hindu-Muslim unity directly, if the Hindus had devoted themselves to national work, the Mahomedans would have gradually come of themselves.... This attempt to patch up a unity has given too much importance to the Muslims and it has been the root of all these troubles.

*
* *

**August 3, 1926**

Religion is as much useful and in the same manner as any other form of culture, e.g., art, science, ethics, etc. All these help the development of man; they prepare the materials which will enrich his higher spiritual life.... But as the other departments of culture—aesthetics, morals, science—can be abused, so religion also can be abused and in fact is very often abused. And as it is said, when the best thing degenerates it becomes the worst corruption—so it is with religion; when its great possibilities are abused it leads to the worst evils.

* * *

**August 4, 1926**

*(A disciple:) Religion is too complex a phenomenon to be defined. The Bengali equivalent of religion—dharma —is still more complex.*

Dharma is not religion though it has become customary to translate "religion" by "dharma." Dharma is law—it includes the social and moral laws; also the law of one's own being, one's own nature is said to be dharma—*svadharma*.

* * *

**August 7, 1926**

*(A disciple:) What are the characteristics of Indian politicians?*

They never do a thing at the right time and whatever they do, they do badly *(laughter)*. They have no touch with reality —they see what the English people are doing in England and try to apply that to this country, though it may be quite unsuitable here. They take all political cants and catch phrases and they adopt them in their talk, not in work. They have too much mental activity—have all sorts of ideas and forms in their brains, which have very little practical value.

*Why is this so?*

That is all due to Mayavada [the doctrine of Illusion]—our men have become too subtle in their minds and all our politicians are drawn from that class. Then the system of education is greatly responsible for this state of things.

*Is the system in England different from that introduced in India?*

Yes, [in India] they want only clerks and the education is intended for nothing else.

*\* \**

**August 8, 1926**

The Greeks had more light than the Christians who converted them; at that time there was gnosticism in Greece, and they were developing agnosticism and so forth. The Christians brought darkness rather than light.

That has always been the case with aggressive religions —they tend to overrun the earth. Hinduism on the other hand is passive and therein lies its danger....

*(A disciple:) There is a marked difference between the national workers of the Swadeshi period and those at the present time. The former workers drew their inspiration from the Gita; the present workers have discarded the Gita, they laugh at spirituality, they draw their inspiration from the Bolshevists or similar other European movements.*

That is the reason why they have degenerated and cannot do anything. They only take the forms adopted in the previous movement without realizing the changed circumstances and fresh requirements of the time.

*Most of our workers and leaders at the present time are without any spiritual life.*

I cannot say anything about individuals. But the central thing in Hinduism is spirituality and there cannot be any big movement without any spirituality behind it.

\*
\* \*

**Early August, 1926**

*(A disciple:) If this work of bringing down the Truth does not succeed in India, do you think India will lose the chance for ever?*

India has the greatest chance because of her past and because the spiritual force is accumulated here....

But if India remains indifferent and sticks to old worn-out forms and refuses to move forward or listen to the call of her soul, then the Truth may recede and try somewhere else. The Truth is not confined to India, it is not India's property. But there is very little chance of its succeeding elsewhere if it fails in India. It may make an unsuccessful or partially successful effort somewhere else, as Christianity did, and then retire.

\*
\* \*

**August 21, 1926**

I find it always difficult to work [innerly] in Indian politics. The difficulty is that the vessels don't hold the Power, they are so weak. If the amount of force that is spent on India were spent on a European nation you would find it full of creative activities of various kinds. But here, in India, it is like sending a current of electricity through a sleeping man: he suddenly starts up, begins jerking and throwing his arms and feet about and then drops down again; he is not fully awake.

*(A disciple:) What is it due to?*

Due to tremendous tamas. Don't you feel it all around, that tamas? It is that which frustrates all efforts.

*What has brought it about?*

It is the result of various causes. It was already settling—I mean, the forces of disintegration and inertia—before the British came. And after their coming the whole tamas has settled like a solid block. There must be some awakening before something substantial can be done. Otherwise, India has got very good men; you had Tilak, Das, Vivekananda —none of them an ordinary man, and yet you see the tamas there.

*\* \* \**

**August 29, 1926**

*(Sri Aurobindo refuted a criticism of birth control in an article.)*

Scientists and medical men have devised methods by which birth control may be made effective without any injury. The objects are twofold: first, the prevention of too many children; secondly, keeping the woman in good health, so that the few children she gives birth to may be healthy.

Of course inner control is better. But can that be expected of the man?...

*(A disciple:) Gandhi has quoted all the doctors who oppose this method.*

But he has not quoted those who support it.

*One objection is that it will increase licence.*

That again is the moralist idea. There are the two extremes: one extreme is inner control, the other is free indulgence; mid-between comes the system of birth control.

*\* \**

**September 6, 1926**

All the energy that I have I owe to yoga. I was very incapable before. Even the energy that I put forth in politics came from yoga.

*\* \**

# IV

## 1929 — 1938

*(At the end of 1926, Sri Aurobindo withdrew com-
pletely, leaving the material responsibility of the
disciples and the growing Ashram to Mother. Apart
from three and later four yearly "darshans," Sri
Aurobindo kept in external touch with the disciples
through letters—thousands of letters in which he
tirelessly dealt with their questions or difficulties or
revolts.*

*This section consists mostly of excerpts from some
of Sri Aurobindo's letters.)*

## Undated

Man is a transitional being; he is not final....
The step from man to superman is the next approaching achievement in the earth's evolution. It is inevitable because it is at once the intention of the inner Spirit and the logic of Nature's process....
Supermanhood is not man climbed to his own natural zenith, not a superior degree of human greatness, knowledge, power, intelligence, will, character, genius, dynamic force, saintliness, love, purity or perfection. Supermind is something beyond mental man and his limits; it is a greater consciousness than the highest consciousness proper to human nature.

Man in himself is little more than an ambitious nothing. He is a littleness that reaches to a wideness and a grandeur that are beyond him, a dwarf enamoured of the heights. His mind is a dark ray in the splendours of the universal Mind. His life is a striving, exulting, suffering, an eager passion-tossed and sorrow-stricken or a blindly and dumbly longing petty moment of the universal Life. His body is a labouring perishable speck in the material universe. This cannot be the end of the mysterious upward surge of Nature. There is something beyond, something that mankind shall be.[89]

*

The world is not either a creation of Maya or only a play, _lilā_, of the Divine, or a cycle of births in the ignorance from which we have to escape, but a field of manifestation in which there is a progressive evolution of the soul and the nature in Matter and from Matter through Life and Mind to what is beyond Mind till it reaches the complete revelation of Sachchidananda* in life. It is this that is the basis of [Sri Aurobindo's] Yoga and gives a new sense to life.[90]

---

* _Sachchidananda:_ the eternal divine principle of Existence (_sat_), Consciousness (_chit_) and Delight (_ānanda_).

**October 23, 1929**

*(From a letter to a Muslim disciple who started
making violent demands which he tried to justify
on "religious" grounds.)*

You say that you ask only for the Truth and yet you speak like a narrow and ignorant fanatic who refuses to believe in anything but the religion in which he was born. All fanaticism is false, because it is a contradiction of the very nature of God and of Truth. Truth cannot be shut up in a single book, Bible or Veda or Koran, or in a single religion. The Divine Being is eternal and universal and infinite and cannot be the sole property of the Mussulmans or of the Semitic religions only,—those that happened to be in a line from the Bible and to have Jewish or Arabian prophets for their founders. Hindus and Confucians and Taoists and all others have as much right to enter into relation with God and find the Truth in their own way. All religions have some truth in them, but none has the whole truth; all are created in time and finally decline and perish. Mahomed himself never pretended that the Koran was the last message of God and there would be no other. God and Truth outlast these religions and manifest themselves anew in whatever way or form the Divine Wisdom chooses. You cannot shut up God in the limitations of your own narrow brain or dictate to the Divine Power and Consciousness how or where or through whom it shall manifest; you cannot put up your puny barriers against the divine Omnipotence. These again are simple truths which are now being recognised all over the world; only the childish in mind or those who vegetate in some formula of the past deny them.

You have insisted on my writing and asked for the Truth and I have answered. But if you want to be a Mussulman, no one prevents you. If the Truth I bring is too great for you to understand or to bear, you are free to go and live in a half-truth or in your own ignorance. I am not here to convert anyone; I do not preach to the world to come to me and I call no one. I am here to establish the divine life and the divine consciousness in those who of themselves feel the call to come to me and cleave to it and in no others.[91]

*
* *

**January 14, 1932**

The traditions of the past are very great in their own place, in the past, but I do not see why we should merely repeat them and not go farther. In the spiritual development of the consciousness upon earth the great past ought to be followed by a greater future.

...

I am concerned with the earth, not with worlds beyond for their own sake; it is a terrestrial realisation that I seek and not a flight to distant summits.[92]

*
* *

**July 31, 1932**

*(From an unpublished letter.)*

As for Gandhi, why should you suppose that I am so tender for the faith of the Mahatma? I do not call it faith at all, but a rigid mental belief and what he calls soul-force is only a strong vital will which has taken a religious turn. That, of course, can be a tremendous force for action, but unfortunately Gandhi spoils it by his ambition to be a man of reason, while in fact he has no reason in him at all, never was reasonable at any moment in his life and, I suppose, never will be. What he has in its place is a remarkable type of unintentionally sophistic logic. Well, what this reason, this amazingly precisely unreliable logic brings about is that nobody is even sure and, I don't think, he is himself really sure what he will do next.* He has not only two minds but three or four minds, and all depends on which will turn up topmost at a particular moment and how it will combine with the others. There would be no harm in that, on the contrary these might be an advantage if there were a central Light somewhere choosing for him and shaping the decision to the need of the action. He thinks there is and calls it God—but it has always seemed to me that it is his own mind that decides and most often decides wrongly. Anyhow I cannot imagine Lenin or Mustapha Kemal not knowing their own minds or acting in this way—even their strategic retreats were steps towards an end clearly conceived and executed. But whatever it be it is all mind action and vital force in Gandhi. So why should he be taken as an example of the defeat of the Divine or of a spiritual Power?** I quite allow that there has been something behind Gandhi greater than himself and you can call it the Divine or a Cosmic Force which has used him, but then there is that behind everybody who is used as an instrument for world ends,—behind Kemal and Lenin also; so that is not germane to the matter.

*
* *

----

* This was also noted by many of those who approached Gandhi. Nehru, for instance, wrote: "I told him [Gandhi, in March, 1931] that his way of springing surprises upon us frightened me, there was something unknown about him which, in spite of the closest association for fourteen years, I could not understand at all and which filled me with apprehension. He admitted the presence of this unknown in him, and said that he himself could not answer for it or foretell what it might lead to."[93]

** The disciple had probably referred to the second Round Table Conference, which Gandhi attended in London at the end of 1931 and which ended in failure. The British government in response unleashed a reign of terror, caning and firing on demonstrators, jailing, whipping and torturing tens of thousands. It then promulgated its "Communal Award," which further hardened the division between Hindus and Muslims, also among the Hindus on the basis of caste.

**August 30, 1932**

[The Mother and myself] do not found ourselves on faith alone, but on a great ground of knowledge which we have been developing and testing all our lives. I think I can say that I have been testing day and night for years upon years more scrupulously than any scientist his theory or his method on the physical plane. That is why I am not alarmed by the aspect of the world around me or disconcerted by the often successful fury of the adverse Forces who increase in their rage as the Light comes nearer and nearer to the field of earth and Matter.[94]

\* \*

**May, 1933**

... But what a floundering confusion the intellect of man has brought itself into now-a-days—whether in thought or in the field of practical life! An infant crying in the night when he is not hitting other infants in the stomach in order to bring the *golden age*. (I am referring to infants like Hitler, Mussolini and others.)[95]

\* \*

**August 10, 1933**

*(A disciple:) I am disconcerted at what is happening in the world. Everywhere misery is rampant, people are losing faith in everything and even the intellectuals like Tagore, Russell and Rolland are clamouring for an end of the age....*

Even if all smashed, I would look beyond the smash to the new creation. As for what is happening in the world, it does not upset me because I knew all along that things would happen in that fashion, and as for the hopes of the intellectual idealists I have not shared them, so I am not disappointed.[96]

\* \* \*

## January 14, 1934

[The aim of the yoga I practise] is to manifest, reach or embody a higher consciousness upon earth and not to get away from earth into a higher world or some supreme Absolute. The old yogas (not quite all of them) tended the other way —but that was, I think, because they found the earth as it is a rather impossible place for any spiritual being and the resistance to change too obstinate to be borne.... But the fundamental proposition in this matter was proclaimed very definitely in the Upanishads which went so far as to say that Earth is the foundation\* and all the worlds are on the earth and to imagine a clean-cut or irreconcilable difference between them is ignorance: here and not elsewhere, not by going to some other world, the divine realisation must come.[97]

\* \* \*

## March 24, 1934

Tagore, of course, belonged to an age which had faith in its ideas and whose very denials were creative affirmations.... Now all that idealism has been smashed to pieces by the immense adverse event and everybody is busy exposing its weaknesses—but nobody knows what to put in its place. A mixture of scepticism and slogans, "Heil-Hitler" and the Fascist salute and the Five-Year-Plan and the beating of everybody into one amorphous shape, a disabused denial of all ideals on one side and on the other a blind "shut-my-eyes

---

\* "Earth is his footing" (Brihadaranyaka Upanishad, I.1.1), "in matter he has taken his firm foundation" (Mundaka Upanishad, II.2.8).

and shut-everybody's-eyes" plunge into the bog in the hope of finding some firm foundation there, will not carry us very far. And what else is there? Until new spiritual values are discovered, no great enduring creation is possible.[98]

* * *

**Undated (1934)**

As for the Hindu-Muslim affair, I saw no reason why the greatness of India's past or her spirituality should be thrown into the waste paper basket in order to conciliate the Moslems who would not at all be conciliated by such policy. What has created the Hindu-Moslem split was not Swadeshi, but the acceptance of the communal principle by the Congress (here Tilak made his great blunder), and the further attempt by the Khilafat movement to conciliate them and bring them in on wrong lines. The recognition of that communal principle at Lucknow made them permanently a separate political entity in India which ought never to have happened; the Khilafat affair made that separate political entity an organised separate political power.[99] *

* * *

**October 2, 1934**

I do not care a button about having my name in any blessed place. I was never ardent about fame even in my political days; I preferred to remain behind the curtain, push people

---

* Tilak, released in 1914 from a six-year-long deportation to Burma, launched in 1916 the Home Rule agitation and led a few months later the reentry of the Nationalists into the Congress at its Lucknow session. The Muslim League also met at Lucknow at the same time, and agreed to work with the Congress in exchange for the concession of separate electorates and fixed numbers of seats for Muslims in the Provincial and Imperial Legislative Councils (the so-called "Lucknow Pact").

without their knowing it and get things done. It was the confounded British Government that spoiled my game by prose-
cuting me and forcing me to be publicly known and a "leader".
Then, again, I don't believe in advertisement except for books
etc., and in propaganda except for politics and patent medi-
cines. But for serious work it is a poison. It means either a
stunt or a boom—and stunts and booms exhaust the thing
they carry on their crest and leave it lifeless and broken high
and dry on the shores of nowhere—or it means a movement.
A movement in the case of a work like mine means the founding of a school or a sect or some other damned nonsense. It
means that hundreds or thousands of useless people join in
and corrupt the work or reduce it to a pompous farce from
which the Truth that was coming down recedes into secrecy
and silence. It is what has happened to the "religions" and is
the reason of their failure. If I tolerate a little writing about
myself, it is only to have a sufficient counter-weight in that
amorphous chaos, the public mind, to balance the hostility
that is always aroused by the presence of a new dynamic
Truth in this world of ignorance. But the utility ends there
and too much advertisement would defeat that object. I am
perfectly "rational", I assure you, in my methods and I do
not proceed merely on any personal dislike of fame. If and so
far as publicity serves the Truth, I am quite ready to tolerate
it; but I do not find publicity for its own sake desirable.[100]

*
* *

**Undated**

It is not by these means [modern humanism and humanitarianism, idealism, etc.] that humanity can get that radical
change of its ways of life which is yet becoming imperative,
but only by reaching the bed-rock of Reality behind,—not
through mere ideas and mental formations, but by a change
of the consciousness, an inner and spiritual conversion. But

that is a truth for which it would be difficult to get a hearing in the present noise of all kinds of many-voiced clamour and confusion and catastrophe.

...

Science has missed something essential; it has seen and scrutinised what has happened and in a way how it has happened, but it has shut its eyes to something that made this impossible possible, something it is there to express. There is no fundamental significance in things if you miss the Divine Reality; for you remain embedded in a huge surface crust of manageable and utilisable appearance. It is the magic of the Magician you are trying to analyse, but only when you enter into the consciousness of the Magician himself can you begin to experience the true origination, significance and circles of the Lila.

...

Another danger may then arise [once materialism begins to give way]—not of a final denial of the Truth, but the repetition in old or new forms of a past mistake, on one side some revival of blind fanatical obscurantist sectarian religionism, on the other a stumbling into the pits and quagmires of the vitalistic occult and the pseudo-spiritual—mistakes that made the whole real strength of the materialistic attack on the past and its credos. But these are phantasms that meet us always on the border line or in the intervening country between the material darkness and the perfect Splendour. In spite of all, the victory of the supreme Light even in the darkened earth-consciousness stands as the one ultimate certitude.[101]

*

I find it difficult to take these psycho-analysts at all seriously when they try to scrutinise spiritual experience by the flicker of their torch-lights,—yet perhaps one ought to, for half-knowledge is a powerful thing and can be a great obstacle to the coming in front of the true Truth. This new psychology looks to me very much like children learning some summary and not very adequate alphabet, exulting in putting their a-b-c-d of the subconscient and the mysterious underground super-ego together and imagining that their first book of obscure beginnings (c-a-t cat, t-r-e-e tree) is the very heart of the real knowledge. They look from down up and explain the higher lights by the lower obscurities; but the foundation of these things is above and not below, *upari budhna esām* [*Rig-Veda*, 1.24.7]. The superconscient, not the subconscient, is the true foundation of things. The significance of the lotus is not to be found by analysing the secrets of the mud from which it grows here; its secret is to be found in the heavenly archetype of the lotus that blooms for ever in the Light above. The self-chosen field of these psychologists is besides poor, dark and limited; you must know the whole before you can know the part and the highest before you can truly understand the lowest. That is the promise of the greater psychology awaiting its hour before which these poor gropings will disappear and come to nothing.[102]

*

Wanton waste, careless spoiling of physical things in an incredibly short time, loose disorder, misuse of service and materials due either to vital grasping or to tamasic inertia are baneful to prosperity and tend to drive away or discourage the Wealth-Power. These things have long been rampant in the society and, if that continues, an increase in our means might well mean a proportionate increase in the wastage and disorder and neutralise the material advantage. This must be remedied if there is to be any sound progress.

Asceticism for its own sake is not the ideal of this yoga, but self-control in the vital and right order in the material are a very important part of it—and even an ascetic discipline is better for our purpose than a loose absence of true control. Mastery of the material does not mean having plenty and profusely throwing it out or spoiling it as fast as it comes or faster. Mastery implies in it the right and careful utilisation of things and also a self-control in their use.[103]

*

There is a consciousness in [things], a life which is not the life and consciousness of man and animal which we know, but still secret and real. That is why we must have a respect for physical things and use them rightly, not misuse and waste, ill-treat or handle with a careless roughness. This feeling of all being consciousness or alive comes when our own physical consciousness—and not the mind only—awakes out of its obscurity and becomes aware of the One in all things, the Divine everywhere.[104]

*
* *

**December 25, 1934**

As to whether the Divine seriously means something to happen, I believe it is intended. I know with absolute certitude that the supramental is a truth and that its advent is in the very nature of things inevitable. The question is as to the when and the how. That also is decided and predestined from somewhere above; but it is here being fought out amid a rather grim clash of conflicting forces. For in the terrestrial world the predetermined result is hidden and what we see is a whirl of possibilities and forces attempting to achieve something with the destiny of it all concealed from human eyes. This is, however, certain that a number of souls have been sent to see that it shall be now. That is the situation. My faith and will are for the now.[105]

*
* *

**January 25, 1935**

I know it is the Russian explanation of the recent trend to spirituality and mysticism that it is a phenomenon of capitalist society in its decadence. But to read an economic cause, conscious or unconscious, into all phenomena of man's history is part of the Bolshevik gospel born of the fallacy of Karl Marx. Man's nature is not so simple and one-chorded as all that—it has many lines and each line produces a need of his life. The spiritual or mystic line is one of them and man tries to satisfy it in various ways, by superstitions of all kinds, by ignorant religionism, by spiritism, demonism and what not, in his more enlightened parts by spiritual philosophy, the higher occultism and the rest, at his highest by the union with the All, the Eternal or the Divine.... With the deeper minds the dissatisfaction with the ideals of the past or the present, with all mental or vital or material solutions of the problem of life has increased and only the spiritual path is left. It is true that the European mind having little light on these things dallies with vital will-o'-the-wisps like spiritism or theosophy or falls back upon the old religionism; but the deeper minds of which I speak either pass by them or pass through them in search of a greater Light....[106]

\* \*

**February 10, 1935**

It is not for personal greatness that I am seeking to bring down the Supermind. I care nothing for greatness or littleness in the human sense. I am seeking to bring some principle of inner Truth, Light, Harmony, Peace into the earth-consciousness; I see it above and know what it is—I feel it ever gleaming down on my consciousness from above and I am seeking to make it possible for it to take up the whole being into its own native power, instead of the nature of man continuing to remain in half-light, half-darkness. I believe the descent of this Truth opening the way to a development of divine consciousness here to be the final sense of the earth evolution.[107]

* * *

**August 8, 1935**

From the spiritual point of view such temporary phenomena as the turn of the educated Hindus towards materialism are of little importance. There have always been periods when the mind of nations, continents or cultures turned towards materialism and away from all spiritual belief.... These waves come because of a certain necessity in human development—to destroy the bondage of old forms and leave a field for new truth and new forms of truth and action in life as well as for what is behind life.[108]

* * *

**August 18, 1935**

I regard the spiritual history of mankind and especially of India as a constant development of a divine purpose, not a book that is closed and the lines of which have to be constantly repeated. Even the Upanishads and the Gita were not final though everything may be there in seed.... I may say that it is far from my purpose to propagate any religion, new or old, for humanity in the future. A way to be opened that is still blocked, not a religion to be founded, is my conception of the matter.[109]

* * *

**Undated**

Human reason is a very convenient and accommodating instrument and works only in the circle set for it by interest, partiality and prejudice. The politicians reason wrongly or insincerely and have power to enforce the results of their reasoning so as to make a mess of the world's affairs: the intellectuals reason and show what their minds show them, which is far from being always the truth, for it is generally decided by intellectual preference and the mind's inborn education-inculcated angle of vision; but even when they see it, they have no power to enforce it. So between blind power and seeing impotence the world moves, achieving destiny through a mental muddle.[110]

*

War and conquest are part of the economy of vital Nature, it is no use blaming this or that people for doing it—everybody does it who has the power and the chance. China who now complains was herself an imperialist and colonising country through all the centuries in which Japan kept religiously within her own borders.... If it were not profitable, I suppose nobody would do it. England has grown rich on the plundered wealth of India. France depends for many things on her African colonies. Japan needs an outlet for her over-abundant population and safe economic markets nearby. Each is pushed by forces that use the minds of rulers and peoples to fulfil themselves—unless human nature changes no amount of moralizing will prevent it.[111]

*
* *

**September 10, 1935**

There is no connection between the spiritual truth and knowledge in which I live and Mahatma Gandhi's ideals and ways of life. If it were so, then I would have to live like him—for surely you do not suppose that my truth and knowledge are only in the mind and are not intended to have a practical manifestation in life! I have always written that my Yoga is intended for the manifestation of a new principle of life and works are an essential part of my Yoga. If that manifestation were already there, there would be no need for my bringing down into life this new spiritual principle. Mahatma Gandhi's life expresses his own ideas of the true truth and the true knowledge. These ideas are not mine.*

The principle of life which I seek to establish is spiritual. Morality is a question of man's mind and vital, it belongs to a lower plane of consciousness. A spiritual life therefore cannot be founded on a moral basis, it must be founded on a spiritual basis. This does not mean that the spiritual man must be immoral—as if there were no other law of conduct than the moral. The law of action of the spiritual conscious-ness is higher not lower than the moral,—it is founded on union with the Divine and living in the Divine Consciousness and its action is founded on obedience to the Divine Will.[112]

*
* *

**September 16, 1935**

*(A disciple:) It is rather depressing to hear about the atrocities committed by some Mohamedans on Hindu families in Bengal. With the coming of Independence I hope such things will stop.... In your scheme of things do you definitely see a free India?...*

That is all settled. It is a question of working out only. The question is what is India going to do with her Independence? The above kind of affair? Bolshevism? Goonda-raj? Things look ominous.[113]

*
* *

---

* This first paragraph is published here for the first time.

**October 8, 1935**

If going beyond the experiences of past seers and sages is so shocking, each new seer or sage in turn has done that shocking thing—Buddha, Shankara, Chaitanya, etc. all did that wicked act.... Truly, this shocked reverence for the past is a wonderful and fearful thing! After all, the Divine is infinite and the unrolling of the Truth may be an infinite process or at least, if not quite so much, yet with some room for new discovery and new statement, even perhaps new achievement, not a thing in a nutshell cracked and its contents exhausted once for all by the first seer or sage, while the others must religiously crack the same nutshell all over again, each tremblingly fearful not to give the lie to the "past" seers and sages.[114]

*
* *

**October 17, 1935**

There is nothing noble besides in fanaticism—there is no nobility of motive, though there may be a fierce enthusiasm of motive. Religious fanaticism is something psychologically low-born and ignorant—and usually in its action fierce, cruel and base. Religious ardour like that of the martyr who sacrifices himself only is a different thing.[115]

*

**October 19, 1935**

*(A disciple sought Sri Aurobindo's comments on the following statement of Gandhi in response to a call by Dr. B. R. Ambedkar for mass conversions among the depressed classes: "But religion is not like a house or a cloak which can be changed at will. It is more an integral part of one's self than of one's body. Religion*

*is the tie that binds one to one's Creator, and while
the body perishes as it has to, religion persists
even after that.")*

If it is meant by the statement that the form of religion is something permanent and unchangeable, then it cannot be accepted. But if religion here means one's way of communion with the Divine, then it is true that that is something belonging to the inner being and cannot be changed like a house or a cloak for the sake of some personal, social or worldly convenience. If a change is to be made, it can only be for an inner spiritual reason, because of some development from within. No one can be bound to any form of religion or any particular creed or system, but if he changes the one he has accepted for another, for external reasons, that means he has inwardly no religion at all and both his old and his new religion are only an empty formula. At bottom that is I suppose what the statement drives at. Preference for a different approach to the Truth or the desire of inner spiritual self-expression are not the motives of the recommendation of change to which objection is made by the Mahatma here; the object proposed [by Dr. Ambedkar] is an enhancement of social status and consideration which is no more a spiritual motive than conversion for the sake of money or marriage. If a man has no religion in himself, he can change his credal profession for any motive; if he has, he cannot; he can only change it in response to an inner spiritual need. If a man has a bhakti for the Divine in the form of Krishna, he can't very well say, "I will swap Krishna for Christ so that I may become socially respectable." [116]

\*
\* \*

**May 17, 1936**

There is no necessity to reveal one's plans and movements to those who have no business to know it, who are incapable of understanding or who would act as enemies or spoil all as a result of their knowledge.... No moral or spiritual law commands us to make ourselves naked to the world or open up our hearts and minds for public inspection. Gandhi talked about secrecy being a sin but that is one of his many extravagances.[117]

*
* *

**September 13, 1936**

No doubt, hatred and cursing are not the proper attitude. It is true also that to look upon all things and all people with a calm and clear vision, to be uninvolved and impartial in one's judgments is a quite proper yogic attitude. A condition of perfect *samatā* [equanimity] can be established in which one sees all as equal, friends and enemies included, and is not disturbed by what men do or by what happens. The question is whether this is all that is demanded from us. If so, then the general attitude will be of a neutral indifference to everything. But the Gita, which strongly insists on a perfect and absolute *samatā*, goes on to say, "Fight, destroy the adversary, conquer." If there is no kind of general action wanted, no loyalty to Truth as against Falsehood except for one's personal sadhana, no will for the Truth to conquer, then the *samatā* of indifference will suffice. But here there is a work to be done, a Truth to be established against which immense forces are arrayed, invisible forces which can use visible things and persons and actions for their instruments. If one is among the disciples, the seekers of this Truth, one has to take sides for the Truth, to stand against the forces that attack it and seek to stifle it. Arjuna wanted not to stand for either side, to refuse any action of hostility even against assailants; Sri Krishna, who insisted so much on *samatā*, strongly rebuked his attitude and insisted equally on his fighting the adversary. "Have *samatā*," he said, "and seeing clearly the Truth, fight." Therefore to take sides with the Truth and to refuse to concede anything to the Falsehood that attacks, to be unflinchingly loyal and against the hostiles and the attackers, is not inconsistent with equality.... It is a spiritual battle inward and outward; by neutrality and compromise or even passivity one may allow the enemy force to pass and crush down the Truth and its children. If you look at it from this point, you will see that if the inner spiritual equality is right, the active loyalty and firm taking of sides is as right, and the two cannot be incompatible.[118]

\*
\* \*

## September 19, 1936

I do not take the same view of the Hindu religion as Jawaharlal [Nehru]. Religion is always imperfect because it is a mixture of man's spirituality with his endeavours that come in in trying to sublimate ignorantly his lower nature. Hindu religion appears to me as a cathedral-temple, half in ruins, noble in the mass, often fantastic in detail but always fantastic with a significance—crumbling or badly outworn in places, but a cathedral-temple in which service is still done to the Unseen and its real presence can be felt by those who enter with the right spirit. The outer social structure which it built for its approach is another matter.[119]

\*
\* \*

## December 24, 1936

The view taken by the Mahatma in these matters is Christian rather than Hindu—for the Christian, self-abasement, humility, the acceptance of a low status to serve humanity or the Divine are things which are highly spiritual and the noblest privilege of the soul. This view does not admit any hierarchy of castes; the Mahatma accepts castes but on the basis that all are equal before the Divine; a Bhangi [scavenger] doing his dharma is as good as the Brahmin doing his, there is division of function but no hierarchy of functions. That is one view of things and the hierarchic view is another, both having a standpoint and logic of their own which the mind takes as wholly valid but which only corresponds to a part of the reality. All kinds of work are equal before the Divine and all men have the same Brahman within them is one truth, but that development is not equal in all is another. The idea that it needs a special *punya* to be born as a Bhangi is, of course, one of those forceful exaggerations of an idea which are common with the Mahatma and impress greatly the mind of his hearers. The idea behind is that his function is an indispensable service to the society, quite as much as the Brahmin's, but, that being disagreeable, it would need a special moral heroism to choose it voluntarily and he thinks as if the soul freely chose it as such a heroic service and as reward of righteous acts—but that is hardly likely. The service of the scavenger is indispensable under certain conditions of society, it is one of those primary necessities without which society can hardly exist and the cultural development of which the Brahmin life is part could not have taken place. But obviously the cultural development is more valuable than the service of the physical needs for the progress of humanity as opposed to its first static condition, and that development can even lead to the minimising and perhaps the entire disappearance by scientific inventions of the need for the functions of the scavenger. But that, I suppose, the Mahatma would not approve of, as it would come by machinery and would be a departure from the simple life. In any case, it is not true that the Bhangi life is superior to the Brahmin life and the reward of a special righteousness. On the other hand, the traditional conception that a man is superior to others because he is born a Brahmin is not rational or justifiable. A spiritual or cultured man of pariah birth is superior in the divine values to an unspiritual and worldly-minded or a crude and uncultured Brahmin. Birth counts, but the basic value is in the man himself, in the soul behind, and the degree to which it manifests itself in his nature.[120]

*<br>* *

**November 17, 1938**

All this* promises a bad look-out when India gets purna Swaraj. Mahatma Gandhi is having bad qualms about Congress corruption already. What will it be when purna Satyagraha reigns all over India?[121]

*<br>* *

---

* Sri Aurobindo is referring to certain dishonest financial practices.

# V

# 1938 — 1940

*(In the night of November 23-24, 1938, Sri Aurobindo fell down while walking in concentration and broke his right leg. In the years that followed, a small group of disciples, mostly attendants and physicians, met him every day. Two of them recorded the informal talks that ensued, which often touched on the Indian political scene, the rising threat of Nazism, and then World War II which Sri Aurobindo followed closely.*

*A few excerpts from these talks are presented here.)*

**December 23, 1938**

Every time the Light has tried to descend it has met with resistance and opposition. Christ was crucified.... Buddha was denied; sons of Light come, the earth denies them, rejects them, and afterwards accepts them in name to reject them in substance.

* *

**December 25, 1938**

I have no faith in government controls, because I believe in a certain amount of freedom—freedom to find out things for oneself in one's own way, even freedom to commit blunders. Nature leads us through various errors and mistakes; when Nature created the human being with all his possibilities for good and ill she knew very well what she was about. Freedom for experiment in human life is a great thing. Without the freedom to take risks and commit mistakes there can be no progress....

[But] everything is moving towards mechanization in Europe. The totalitarian States do not believe in any individual variation and even non-totalitarian States are obliged to follow them; they do it for the sake of efficiency—but whose efficiency? It is the efficiency of the State as an organized machine, not that of the individual. The individual has no freedom, he doesn't grow. Organize by all means, but there must be scope for freedom and plasticity.

. . .

Do you think that the average man of today is better than a Greek of 2500 hundred years ago, or than an Indian of those times? Look at the condition of Germany today [under Hitler] —you can't say that it is progressing.

I have come in contact with the Indian masses and found them better than the Europeans of the same class. They are superior to the European working classes. The latter may be more efficient, but that is due to external reasons.... The Irish doctor who was in our jail [at Alipore] could not think how the young men who were so gentle and attractive could be revolutionaries. I found even the ordinary criminal quite human and better than his counterpart in Europe.

...

It is curious how a thing gets spoiled when it gets recognition. Democracy was something better when it was not called democracy. When the name is given the truth of it seems to go out....

*(A disciple:) Communism began with a high ideal and it is certainly better than Fascism or Nazism.*

In which way better? Formerly people were unconscious slaves, now under Communism they are conscious slaves.... They are bound to the State, the dictator and the party. They can't even choose the dictator. And whoever differs from them is mercilessly suppressed.... The whole thing—whatever its name—is a fraud. It is impossible to change humanity by political machinery—it can't be done.

*
* *

**December 27, 1938**

The old Indian system grew out of life, it had room for everything and every interest. There were monarchy, aristocracy, democracy; every interest was represented in the government. While in Europe the Western system grew out of the mind: they are led by reason and want to make everything cut and dried without any chance of freedom or variation. If it is democracy, then democracy only—no room for anything else. They cannot be plastic.

India is now trying to imitate the West. Parliamentary government is not suited to India. But we always take up what the West has thrown off....

*(A disciple:) What is your idea of an ideal government for India?*

My idea is like what Tagore once wrote. There may be one Rashtrapati at the top with considerable powers so as to secure a continuity of policy, and an assembly representative of the nation. The provinces will combine into a federation united at the top, leaving ample scope to local bodies to make laws according to their local problems.

. . .

The Congress at the present stage—what is it but a Fascist organization? Gandhi is the dictator like Stalin, I won't say like Hitler: what Gandhi says they accept and even the Working Committee follows him; then it goes to the All-India Congress Commitee which adopts it, and then the Congress. There is no opportunity for any difference of opinion, except for Socialists who are allowed to differ provided they don't seriously differ. Whatever resolutions they pass are obligatory on all the provinces whether the resolutions suit the provinces or not; there is no room for any other independent opinion. Everything is fixed up before and the people are only allowed to talk over it—like Stalin's Parliament. When we started the [Nationalist] movement we began with the idea of throwing out the Congress oligarchy and open the whole organization to the general mass.

*Srinivas Iyengar retired from Congress because of his differences with Gandhi....*

He made Charkha a religious article of faith and excluded all people from Congress membership who could not spin. How many even among his own followers believe in his gospel of Charkha? Such a tremendous waste of energy just for the sake of a few annas is most unreasonable.

...

Give [people] education, technical training and give them the fundamental organic principles of organization, not on political but on business lines. But Gandhi does not want such industrial organization, he is for going back to the old system of civilization, and so he comes in with his magical formula "Spin, spin, spin." C. R. Das and a few others could act as a counterbalance. It is all a fetish.

\* \*

**December 30, 1938**

The Japanese have a wonderful power of self-control. They don't lose their temper or quarrel with you, but if their honour is violated they may kill you. They can be bitter enemies.... The Japanese also have a high sense of chivalry.... But these things perhaps belong to the past. It is a great pity that people who have carried such ideals into practice are losing them through contact with European civilization. That is a great harm that European vulgarizing has done to Japan. Now you find most people mercantile in their outlook and they will do anything for the sake of money.....

*(A disciple:) Has European civilization nothing good in it?*

It has lowered the moral tone of humanity.... The ancients tried to keep to their ideals and made an effort to raise them higher, while Europe lost all her ideals after the [first World] War. People have become cynical, selfish, etc.... I suppose it is all due to commercialism.

\* \*

**January 6, 1939**

Are not all governments robbers? Some do the robbing with legislation, some without.

*<br>* *

**January 8, 1939**

*(A disciple:) Gandhi writes that non-violence tried by some people in Germany has failed because it has not been so strong as to generate sufficient heat to melt Hitler's heart.*

I am afraid it would require quite a furnace!... The trouble with Gandhi is that he had to deal only with Englishmen, and the English want to have their conscience at ease. Besides, the Englishman wants to satisfy his self-esteem and wants world-esteem. But if Gandhi had had to deal with the Russians or the German Nazis, they would have long ago put him out of their way.

*<br>* *

**January 15, 1939**

It is easy to see that the process of evolution is universal and human evolution cannot be bound down to a set of philosophical ideas or rules of practice. No epoch, no individual, no group has the monopoly of truth. It is the same with religion—Christian, Mohammedan, etc.

. . .

The Greeks had the sense of beauty; their life was beautiful. The one thing that modern Europe has not taken from the Greeks is beauty. You can't say modern Europe is beautiful —in fact, it is ugly.

What can be said of ancient Greece can be said also of ancient India. She had beauty, much of which she has since lost. The Japanese are the only race that can be said to have preserved beauty in their life. But now even they are fast losing it under European influence.

The setback to the human mind in Europe is amazing.... We had thought during the last years of the nineteenth century that the human mind had attained a certain level of intelligence and that it would have to be satisfied before any new idea could find acceptance. But it seems one can't rely on common sense to stand the strain. We find Nazi ideas being accepted; fifty years back it would have been impossible to predict their acceptance. Then, again, the ease with which the best intellectuals accept psychoanalysis and Freud's ideas is surprising.
. . .

Throughout the course of history a small minority has been carrying the torch to save humanity in spite of itself.

\*
\* \*

**January 16, 1939**

> *(A disciple:) Nana Saheb Sinde of Baroda has spoken to a youth conference emphasizing the need of military training for the defence of the country. His speech was against the current vogue of non-violence.*

It is good that someone raises his voice like that when efforts are being made to make non-violence the method of solving all problems.... This non-violent resistance I have never been able to fathom.... To change the opponent's heart by passive resistance is something I don't understand....

I am afraid Gandhi has been trying to apply to ordinary life what belongs to spirituality. Non-violence or ahimsa as a spiritual attitude and its practice is perfectly understandable and has a standing of its own. You may not accept it in toto but it has a basis in reality. You can live it in spiritual life, but to apply it to all life is absurd.... It is a principle which can be applied with success if practised on a mass scale, specially by unarmed people like the Indians, because you are left with no other choice. But even when it succeeds it is not that you have changed the heart of the enemy, but that you have made it impossible for him to rule....

What a tremendous generalizer Gandhi is! Passive resistance, charkha and celibacy for all! One can't be a member of the Congress without oneself spinning!

\*
\* \*

### January 18, 1939

There is a spiritual solution which I propose; but it aims at changing the whole basis of human nature. It is not a question of carrying on a movement, nor is it a question of a few years: there can be no real solution unless you establish spirituality as the basis of life.

It is clear that Mind has not been able to change human nature radically. You can go on changing human institutions infinitely and yet the imperfection will break through all your institutions.

\*
\* \*

### January 21, 1939

She [Nivedita] took up politics as a part of Vivekananda's work.... Vivekananda himself had ideas about political work and spells of revolutionary fervour.... It is curious how many Sannyasins at that time thought of India's freedom. *

\*
\* \*

---

* It is noteworthy that one of the very first attempts to overthrow British rule was made in eastern India in the last decades of the eighteenth century by organized groups of Sannyasins.

**January 24, 1939**

*(A disciple:) There are so many difficulties [in finding out the cause of poverty], political, economic, etc.*

I don't think it is so insoluble a problem as all that. If you give the people education—by education I mean proper education, not the modern type—then the problem can be solved. People in England or France don't have the kind of poverty we have in India. That is because of their education —they are not so helpless.
. . .
Modern artists are putting an end to art. Vulgarization everywhere!... When this craze for utility comes, beauty goes to the dogs. This is the modern tendency.

*
* *

**January 26, 1939**

*(A disciple:) [In India] the forests are being depleted of animals.*

The forests have to be preserved and also the wildlife. China destroyed all her forests and the result is that there is flood every year.
. . .
In Socialism you have the State which intervenes at every step with its officials who rob money.... It is the State bureaucracy that dictates the policy irrespective of the good of the commune. In Communism they hold the land as the common property of the whole unit, and each one is entitled to labour and to have his share from the produce.

In India we had a kind of communism in the villages. The whole village was like a big family and the lowest had his right as a member of the family. The washerman, the carpenter, the blacksmith, the barber, all got what they needed. That is the only communism that is practicable. Each such commune can be independent and many such units can be scattered all over the country and they can combine or coordinate their activities for a common purpose.

*
* *

**January 29, 1939**

You know what [C. R.] Das said about criminals? He said, "In my whole legal career I have not met worse types of criminals than in politics."
...
It is better not to destroy the capitalist class as the Socialists want to: they are the source of national wealth. They should be encouraged to spend for the nation. Taxing is all right, but you must increase production, start new industries, and also raise the standard of living; without that if you increase the taxes there will be a state of depression.

*
* *

**February 2, 1939**

Nowadays people want the modern type of democracy—the parliamentary form of government. The parliamentary system is doomed. It has brought Europe to its present sorry pass....
[In India] one should begin with the old Panchayat system in the villages and then work up to the top. The Panchayat system and the guilds are more representative and they have a living contact with people; they are part of the people's ideas. On the contrary, the parliamentary system with local bodies—the municipal councils—is not workable: these councils have no living contact with the people; the councillors make only platform speeches and nobody knows what they

do for three or four years; at the end they reshuffle and rear-range the whole thing, making their own pile during their period of power.

\* \*

**November 28, 1939**

*(A disciple:) X was lamenting over the plight of Bengali Hindus. He says there is a cultural conquest taking place.*

How? Hindus are becoming Muslims?

*No, not religious conquest but cultural, Hindu culture being replaced by Muslim. At schools and colleges, books on Muslim culture are being forced on the students.*

Why don't the Hindus react?

*(Another disciple:) Instead of lamenting they should also organize something.*

Quite so.

\* \*

**December 30, 1939**

*(A disciple:) There are some people who object to "Vande Mataram" as a national song. And some Con-gressmen support the removal of some parts of the song.*

In that case the Hindus should give up their culture.

*The argument is that the song speaks of Hindu gods, like Durga, and that is offensive to the Muslims.*

But it is not a religious song: it is a national song and the Durga spoken of is India as the Mother. Why should not the Muslims accept it? It is an image used in poetry. In the Indian conception of nationality, the Hindu view would naturally be there. If it cannot find a place there, the Hindus may as well be asked to give up their culture. The Hindus don't object to "Allah-ho-Akbar"....

Why should not the Hindu worship his god? Otherwise, the Hindus must either accept Mohammedanism or the European culture or become atheists....

I told C. R. Das [in 1923] that this Hindu-Muslim question must be solved before the Britishers go, otherwise there was a danger of civil war. He also agreed and wanted to solve it....

Instead of doing what was necessary the Congress is trying to flirt with Jinnah, and Jinnah simply thinks that he has to obstinately stick to his terms to get them. The more they try, the more Jinnah becomes intransigent.

*
* *

**January 3, 1940**

*(A disciple:) X who is an I.C.S. is said to be brilliant.*

Then why did he go in for the I.C.S. to waste himself?... In that official routine work all the brilliant qualities are lost. There is no scope for them.

*
* *

**February 5, 1940**

*(A disciple:) Dominion status Subhas Bose calls a compromise; he wants independence.*

It is a compromise on the surface, but it is practically independence; you get all you want without any unnecessary struggle. When you can secede at your will from the British connection, it is practically independence.* Independence is all right if you are prepared for a revolution, but is the country ready for it?

*
* *

**April 2, 1940**

*(Smiling)* Have you seen the report of the All India Sweepers' Conference at Lahore under Sardul Singh's presidentship? They have protested against Jinnah's Muslim India scheme and said that if India was going to be divided they must also have a separate India. I was not quite wrong when I said that barbers also would now start an agitation for an India of their own!...

*
* *

**May 5, 1940**

Now they [the Muslim League] say that they are the sole representatives of the Muslims, and the Government strongly supports them. The Congress is also half-hearted against [the scheme of] Pakistan....

The Congress and other people are shouting old slogans in changed conditions. At one time the Independence cry was all right, but now Dominion status is almost equivalent to that and in time you can be virtually independent. Besides, it is the best chance under the present conditions in opposition to charkha and non-violence....

*(A disciple:) If Hitler invades India, Gandhi will declare we are all non-violent.*

Hitler will be delighted at it.

---

* In 1942, Sri Aurobindo publicly supported the Cripps proposal to grant India Dominion status (see page 237).

*Yes, he will sweep off everybody with machine guns.*
*Gandhi believes he can be converted.*

It is a beautiful idea, but not credible. Does anybody really believe in his non-violence?... Will he face an army with his charkha?

*
* *

**May 17, 1940**

It seems it is not five or six of our people [the Ashram's disciples] but more than half that are in sympathy with Hitler and want him to win.*

*(A disciple, laughing:) Half?*

No, it is not a matter to laugh at. It is a very serious matter. ... If these people want that the Ashram should be dissolved, they can come and tell me and I will dissolve it instead of the police doing it. They have no idea about the world and talk like children. Hitlerism is the greatest menace that the world has ever met—if Hitler wins, do they think India has any chance of being free? It is a well-known fact that Hitler has an eye on India. He is openly talking of world-empire....

I hear K. [a disciple] says that Russia can come now and conquer India. It is this kind of slave mentality that keeps India in bondage. He pretends to spirituality; doesn't he know that the first thing that Stalin will do is to wipe out spirituality from India?...

*
* *

---

* A sympathy shared by many in India at the time, which stemmed from a justified anti-British feeling but veiled the reality of what was at stake.

**May 18, 1940**

*(A disciple:) D. was being jeered at [by other "disci-ples"] for being pro-Ally. When he said he was sad at Holland's defeat, they remarked, "You are pro-Ally?"*

They are glad that Holland was occupied? Very strange, and yet they want freedom for India! That is one thing I can't swallow. How can they have sympathy with Hitler who is destroying other nations, taking away their liberty? It is not only pro-Ally sympathy but sympathy for humanity that they are jeering at.

*
* *

**May 21, 1940**

*(A disciple:) Gandhi writes in the* Harijan *that there is not much to choose betwen Imperialism and Fascism. He finds very little difference.*

There is a big difference. Under Fascism he wouldn't be able to write such things or say anything against the State. He would be shot.

*And he still believes that by non-violence we can defend our country.*

Non-violence can't defend. One can only die by it.

*He believes that by such a death a change of heart can take place in the enemy.*

If it does, it will be after two or three centuries.

*
* *

**May 28, 1940**

Have you read what Gandhi has said in answer to a correspondent? He says that if eight crores of Muslims demand a separate State, what else are the twenty-five crores of Hindus to do but surrender? Otherwise there will be civil war.

*(A disciple:) I hope that is not the type of conciliation he is thinking of.*

Not thinking of it, you say? He has actually said that and almost yielded. If you yield to the opposite party beforehand, naturally they will stick strongly to their claims. It means that the minority will rule and the majority must submit. The minority is allowed its say, "We shall be the ruler and you our servants. Our *harf* [word] will be law; you will have to obey." This shows a peculiar mind. I think this kind of people are a little cracked.

*
* *

**June 17, 1940**

*(The German troops entered Paris a few days earlier; on the 17th Pétain proposed an armistice.)*

*(A disciple:) I think everybody realizes the danger if Hitler occupies France.*

Does India realize it? Everybody seems to be busy with his own interest and none considers anything in the light of the world situation. The Congress Committee is now in session; will it realize the danger?

*(Another disciple:) I think it will.*

Let us hope so. Nehru seems to shut his eyes and calls all these fears a bogey of foreign invasion.

*
* *

**June 18, 1940**

*(A disciple:) Some people in India defend France's peace offer.* *They say, "What can the French do? Their army was being annihilated...."*

That is the typical Indian mentality. That is why India is under subjection. Just because an army has been defeated, must it surrender? Then, will a subject nation always be a subject nation? Won't it fight for freedom?... The greatness lies in not giving up the struggle and refusing to accept the defeat as final.

*
* *

**June 21, 1940**

In Kashmir, the Hindus had all the monopoly. Now if the Muslim demands are acceded to, the Hindus will be wiped out.

*
* *

**June 25, 1940**

The greatest preoccupation of modern man seems to be to find out means of destruction as well as means of escaping destruction....

*(A disciple:) Have you read what Jawaharlal says?*

Yes, that he doesn't think there is the slightest likelihood

---

* Not a "peace offer" but Pétain's capitulation to Hitler.

of a major invasion of India. Only a minor invasion from Afghanistan and such places perhaps?...

*If Nehru says like that, how can we blame [others]? Nehru who is supposed to have international politics at his fingertips!*

All the knowledge most Indian politicians have of the international situation is some illusions about extreme political ideas, which have been shattered everywhere.

\*
\* \*

**July 4, 1940**

*(A disciple:) Gandhi has offered his help through the Viceroy to the British government and asked the British to lay down their arms and practise non-violence.*

He must be a little cracked.

*While asking them to lay down their arms, he wants them to keep up their spirit.*

And be subjected in practice!\*

\*
\* \*

---

\* This refers to an open letter which Gandhi addressed to the British a few days earlier: "I appeal for cessation of hostilities ... because war is bad in essence. You want to kill Nazism. Your soldiers are doing the same work of destruction as the Germans. The only difference is that perhaps yours are not as thorough as the Germans.... I venture to present you with a nobler and a braver way, worthy of the bravest soldiers. I want you to fight Nazism without arms or ... with non-violent arms. I would like you to lay down the arms you have as being useless for saving you or humanity.... Invite Herr Hitler and Signor Mussolini to take what they want of the countries you call your possessions. Let them take possession of your beautiful island with your many beautiful buildings. You will give all these but not your souls nor your minds...." (*Amrita Bazar Patrika*, July 4, 1940, "Method of Non-violence —Mahatma Gandhi's appeal to every Briton.")

**July 7, 1940**

With [Subhas] Bose on one side and Gandhi on the other, future unity will be difficult. If Hindus and Muslims had now made a united demand the Government would have had to submit.*

\* \*

**October 7, 1940**

*(A disciple:) It is because of the British divide-and-rule policy that we can't unite.*

Nonsense! Was there unity in India before the British rule?

*But now since our national consciousness is more developed there is more chance of unity if the British don't bolster up Jinnah and his Muslim claims.*

Does Jinnah want unity?... What he wants is independence for Muslims and if possible rule over India. That is the old spirit.... But why is it expected that Muslims will be so accommodating? Everywhere minorities are claiming their rights. Of course, there may be some Muslims who are different, more nationalistic in outlook: even [Maulana] Azad has his own terms, only he sees Indian unity first and will settle those terms afterwards.

\* \*

**October 12, 1940**

*(A disciple:) But how long can Hitler keep these races*

---

\* To submit to granting independence to a united India, as Britain needed India's cooperation during the War.

*[in the countries he invaded] in subjection? They will
rise in revolt one day.*

What about Poland and Czechoslovakia? They are two of
the most heroic nations in the world and yet what can they
do?...

*The trouble about India is that the British govern-
ment has not kept a single promise so far. So nobody
trusts it.*

The fact is that the British don't trust India to help them if
she is given Dominion status. Otherwise they would have
given it.

*I don't think India will refuse to help if we get some-
thing.*

You think so? I am not sure. What do you think of the left-
wingers, Communists, Subhas Bose, for instance? And it is
not true that they [the British] have given nothing.... They
gave provincial autonomy and didn't exercise any veto power.
It is the Congress that spoiled everything by resigning.* If
without resigning they had put pressure at the Centre they
would have got by now what they want. It is for two reasons
I support the British in this war: first in India's own interest
and secondly for humanity's sake, and the reasons I have
given are external reasons, there are spiritual reasons too.**

*
* *

---

* By resigning from all the provincial ministries in October-November,
1939, as the Congress declared itself unable to lend support to Britain in the
war.
** A few days earlier, Sri Aurobindo issued a public declaration in support
of the Allies (see page 236).

# VI

## 1940 — 1950

*(This section consists of excerpts from writings, letters, and messages.)*

**Early 1940**

At present mankind is undergoing an evolutionary crisis in which is concealed a choice of its destiny.... Man has created a system of civilisation which has become too big for his limited mental capacity and understanding and his still more limited spiritual and moral capacity to utilise and manage, a too dangerous servant of his blundering ego and its appetites....

Because the burden which is being laid on mankind is too great for the present littleness of the human personality and its petty mind and small life-instincts, because it cannot operate the needed change, because it is using this new apparatus and organisation to serve the old infraspiritual and infrarational life-self of humanity, the destiny of the race seems to be heading dangerously, as if impatiently and in spite of itself, under the drive of the vital ego seized by colossal forces which are on the same scale as the huge mechanical organisation of life and scientific knowledge which it has evolved, a scale too large for its reason and will to handle, into a prolonged confusion and perilous crisis and darkness of violent shifting incertitude. Even if this turns out to be a passing phase or appearance and a tolerable structural accommodation is found which will enable mankind to proceed less catastrophically on its uncertain journey, this can only be a respite. For the problem is fundamental and in putting it evolutionary Nature in man is confronting herself with a critical choice which must one day be solved in the true sense if the race is to arrive or even to survive.[122]

*
* *

**July 4, 1940**

*(In this letter, Sri Aurobindo is referring
in particular to the Allies.)*

If the nations or the governments who are blindly the
instruments of the divine forces were perfectly pure and
divine in their processes and forms of action as well as in the
inspiration they receive so ignorantly they would be invincible, because the divine forces themselves are invincible. It
is the mixture in the outward expression that gives to the
Asura the right to defeat them.[123]

*
* *

**September 19, 1940**

*(A message to the Governor of Madras, accompanied
by a contribution. This declaration was Sri Aurobindo's
first public intervention since he withdrew in 1910.)*

We feel that not only is this a battle waged in just self-
defence and in defence of the nations threatened with the
world-domination of Germany and the Nazi system of life,
but that it is a defence of civilisation and its highest attained
social, cultural and spiritual values and of the whole future
of humanity. To this cause our support and sympathy will be
unswerving whatever may happen; we look forward to the
victory of Britain and, as the eventual result, an era of peace
and union among the nations and a better and more secure
world-order.[124]

*
* *

## March 31, 1942

*(The British governement, partly realizing the inevitability of India's future independence and partly under American pressure to secure her support during the war, sent Sir Stafford Cripps to India in March, 1942, with a proposal for dominion status after the war, as a first step towards full independence. Sri Aurobindo sent Cripps the following message.)*

As one who has been a nationalist leader and worker for India's independence, though now my activity is no longer in the political but in the spiritual field, I wish to express my appreciation of all you have done to bring about this offer. I welcome it as an opportunity given to India to determine for herself, and organise in all liberty of choice, her freedom and unity, and take an effective place among the world's free nations. I hope that it will be accepted, and right use made of it, putting aside all discords and divisions.... I offer my public adhesion, in case it can be of any help in your work.[125]*

*
* *

---

* The next day, on April 1, Cripps replied with the following telegram: "I am most touched and gratified by your kind message allowing me to inform India that you who occupy unique position in imagination of Indian youth, are convinced that declaration of His Majesty's Government substantially confers that freedom for which Indian Nationalism has so long struggled."

Sri Aurobindo in addition sent a personal messenger to the Congress to urge them to accept Cripps' proposal; he also sent a telegram to C. Rajagopalachari, in which he said: "... Appeal to you to save India. Formidable danger new foreign domination when old on way to self-elimination." (Japan was then threatening to invade Burma and India; a few days earlier, it had also become known that Subhas Bose was in Germany and, confident of Germany's victory, was trying to organize with its help an anti-British front.)

Sri Aurobindo's advice was ignored: "He has retired from political life, why does he interfere!" said Gandhi to Duraiswamy Iyer, Sri Aurobindo's

. . .

**August 7, 1943**

*(From a talk.)*

It was after Dunkirk that I openly came out with my declaration and gave the contribution openly. If I had believed in appearances I should not have. It is in spite of opposite appearances that you have to act on faith.... If you depend upon reason then you can't know what is Truth....

Our people cannot understand why one who has the Divine consciousness or Brahmic consciousness should take sides in a fight. That is all right if you want to remain in the static Brahman; then you can look upon the whole thing as Maya and it may not exist for you.

But I believe in Brahman siding against Brahman—that the Brahman, I think, has always been doing.... Krishna took sides openly in the Mahabharata and Rama also.

*
* *

**September 3, 1943**

*(From a letter to a disciple.)*

We [Sri Aurobindo and Mother] made it plain in a letter which has been made public that we did not consider the war as a fight between nations and governments (still less between good people and bad people) but between two forces, the Divine and the Asuric. What we have to see is on which side men and nations put themselves; if they put themselves on

messenger. Although Nehru and Rajagopalachari favoured acceptance of Cripps' offer, Gandhi found it unacceptable "because of his opposition to war." Maulana Azad, President of the Congress, also opposed it, and the Congress finally turned it down. Had Cripps' proposal been accepted, the Partition and the blood bath that followed might have been averted, as also the three Indo-Pakistan wars.

the right side, they at once make themselves instruments of the Divine purpose in spite of all defects, errors, wrong movements and actions which are common to human nature and all human collectivities. The victory of one side (the Allies) would keep the path open for the evolutionary forces: the victory of the other side would drag back humanity, degrade it horribly and might lead even, at the worst, to its eventual failure as a race, as others in the past evolution failed and perished. That is the whole question and all other considerations are either irrelevant or of a minor importance. The Allies at least have stood for human values, though they may often act against their own best ideals (human beings always do that); Hitler stands for diabolical values or for human values exaggerated in the wrong way until they become diabolical (e.g. the virtues of the Herrenvolk, the master race). That does not make the English or Americans nations of spotless angels nor the Germans a wicked and sinful race, but as an indicator it has a primary importance.

...

Even if I knew that the Allies would misuse their victory or bungle the peace or partially at least spoil the opportunities opened to the human world by that victory, I would still put my force behind them. At any rate things could not be one-hundredth part as bad as they would be under Hitler. The ways of the Lord would still be open—to keep them open is what matters. Let us stick to the real, the central fact, the need to remove the peril of black servitude and revived barbarism threatening India and the world....

P.S. Ours is a Sadhana which involves not only devotion or union with the Divine or a perception of Him in all things and beings but also action as workers and instruments and a work to be done in the world or a force to be brought in the world under difficult conditions; then one has to see one's way and do what is commanded and support what has to be supported, even if it means war and strife carried on whether through chariots and bows and arrows or tanks and cars and American bombs and planes, in either case *ghoram karma* [a dreadful work, *Gita*, 3.1].... As for violence etc. the old command rings out for us once again after many ages: *"Mayaivaite nihatāh pūrvameva nimittamātram bhava Savyasācin"* [By me and none other already they are slain, become only the occasion, O Arjuna, *Gita*, 11.33].[126]

*       *
*

**Mid-1940s**

*(From a letter.)*

I do not regard business as something evil or tainted, any more than it is so regarded in ancient spiritual India.... All depends on the spirit in which a thing is done, the principles on which it is built and the use to which it is turned. I have done politics and the most violent kind of revolutionary politics, *ghoram karma*, and I have supported war and sent men to it, even though politics is not always or often a very clean occupation nor can war be called a spiritual line of action. But Krishna calls upon Arjuna to carry on war of the most terrible kind and by his example encourage men to do every kind of human work, *sarvakarmāni*. Do you contend that Krishna was an unspiritual man and that his advice to Arjuna was mistaken or wrong in principle?
...
I do not regard the ascetic way of living as indispensable to spiritual perfection or as identical with it. There is the way of spiritual self-mastery and the way of spiritual self-giving and surrender to the Divine, abandoning ego and desire even in the midst of action or of any kind of work or all kinds of work demanded from us by the Divine.... The Indian scriptures and Indian tradition, in the Mahabharata and elsewhere, make room both for the spirituality of the renunciation of life and for the spiritual life of action. One cannot say that one only is

the Indian tradition and that the acceptance of life and works of all kinds, *sarvakarmāni*, is un-Indian, European or western and unspiritual.[127]

* * *

### September, 1945

*(From a letter.)*

About the present human civilisation. It is not this which has to be saved; it is the world that has to be saved and that will surely be done, though it may not be so easily or so soon as some wish or imagine, or in the way that they imagine. The present must surely change, but whether by a destruction or a new construction on the basis of a greater Truth, is the issue. The Mother has left the question hanging and I can only do the same.[128]

* * *

### October 19, 1946

*(From a letter to a disciple who expressed anguish at the widespread horrors perpetrated on Hindus by Muslims in Bengal, notably in Noakhali and Tippera districts, now in Bangladesh; this organized violence —which the British government did nothing to stop— was part of Jinnah's plan of "Direct Action" which was intended to demonstrate the impossibility for Hindus and Muslims to live together, and therefore the inevitability of Pakistan.)*

As regards Bengal, things are certainly very bad; the conditions of the Hindus there are terrible and they may even get worse in spite of the Interim *mariage de convenance* at Delhi.*

---

* A reference to the Interim Government worked out between the British and the Congress, which the Muslim League had just agreed to join.

But we must not let our reaction to it become excessive or suggest despair. There must be at least twenty million Hindus in Bengal and they are not going to be exterminated,—even Hitler with his scientific methods of massacre could not exterminate the Jews who are still showing themselves very much alive and as for Hindu culture, it is not such a weak and fluffy thing as to be easily stamped out; it has lasted through something like five millenniums at least and is going to carry on much longer and has accumulated quite enough power to survive. What is happening did not come to me as a surprise. I foresaw it when I was in Bengal and warned people that it was probable and almost inevitable and that they should be prepared for it. At that time no one attached any value to what I said although some afterwards remembered and admitted, when the trouble first began, that I have been right; only C. R. Das had grave apprehensions and he even told me when he came to Pondicherry that he would not like the British to go out until this dangerous problem had been settled. But I have not been discouraged by what is happening, because I know and have experienced hundreds of times that beyond the blackest darkness there lies for one who is a divine instrument the light of God's victory. I have never had a strong and persistent will for anything to happen in the world—I am not speaking of personal things—which did not eventually happen even after delay, defeat or even disaster. There was a time when Hitler was victorious everywhere and it seemed certain that a black yoke of the Asura would be imposed on the whole world; but where is Hitler now and where is his rule? Berlin and Nuremberg have marked the end of that dreadful chapter in human history. Other blacknesses threaten to overshadow or even engulf mankind, but they too will end as that nightmare has ended.[129]

*
* *

**December 2, 1946**

*(From a letter.)*

Mother India is not a piece of earth; she is a Power, a Godhead, for all nations have such a Devi supporting their separate existence and keeping it in being. Such Beings are as real and more permanently real than the men they influence but they belong to a higher plane, are part of the cosmic consciousness and being and act here on earth by shaping the human consciousness on which they exercise their influence. It is natural for man who sees only his own consciousness individual, national or racial at work and does not see what works upon it and shapes it, to think that all is created by him and there is nothing cosmic and greater behind it.[130]

\*
\* \*

**December 22, 1946**

*(A remark to a disciple on India's political scene.)*

Out of all of them, Patel\* is the only strong man.[131]

\*
\* \*

---

\* Sardar Vallabhbhai Patel (1875-1950), who as India's Home Minister after Independence showed great firmness in negotiating the integration of the princely states, Kashmir's accession to India, and the merger of the Hyderabad state.

**April 9, 1947**

*(From a letter.)*

The difficulties [you feel] are general in the Ashram as well as in the outside world. Doubt, discouragement, diminution or loss of faith, waning of the vital enthusiasm for the ideal, perplexity and a baffling of the hope for the future are the common features of the difficulty. In the world outside there are much worse symptoms such as the general increase of cynicism, a refusal to believe in anything at all, a decrease of honesty, an immense corruption, a preoccupation with food, money, comfort, pleasure to the exclusion of higher things and a general expectation of worse and worse things awaiting the world. All that, however acute, is a temporary phenomenon for which those who know anything about the workings of the world-energy and the workings of the Spirit were prepared. I myself foresaw that this worst would come, the darkness of night before dawn; therefore I am not discouraged. I know what is preparing behind the darkness and can see and feel the first signs of its coming. Those who seek for the Divine have to stand firm and persist in their seeking; after a time, the darkness will fade and begin to disappear and the Light will come.[132]

*\* \* \**

**August 15, 1947**

*(A passage from Sri Aurobindo's message on the occasion of India's independence. August 15 is also Sri Aurobindo's own birthday.)*

India is free but she has not achieved unity, only a fissured and broken freedom.... The old communal division into Hindu and Muslim seems to have hardened into the figure of a permanent political division of the country. It is to be hoped that the Congress and the nation will not accept the settled fact as for ever settled or as anything more than a temporary expedient. For if it lasts, India may be seriously weakened, even crippled: civil strife may remain always possible, possible even a new invasion and foreign conquest. The partition of the country must go,—it is to be hoped by a slackening of tension, by a progressive understanding of the need of peace and concord, by the constant necessity of common and concerted action, even of an instrument of union for that purpose. In this way unity may come about under whatever form—the exact form may have a pragmatic but not a fundamental importance. But by whatever means, the division must and will go. For without it the destiny of India might be seriously impaired and even frustrated. But that must not be.[133]*

*
* *

**1947 (?)**

*(From notes to biographers.)*

The idea of two nationalities in India is only a newly-fangled notion invented by Jinnah for his purposes and contrary to the facts. More than 90% of the Indian Mussalmans are descendants of converted Hindus and belong as much to the Indian nation as the Hindus themselves. This process of conversion has continued all along; Jinnah is himself a descendant of a Hindu, converted in fairly recent times, named Jinahbhai and many of the most famous Mohammedan leaders have a similar origin.[134]

*

---

* Newly created Pakistan invaded Kashmir two months later. The Indian army was able to repulse the attack and was about to drive Pakistani forces out of Kashmir when Nehru called a halt to the fighting and brought the "dispute" before the United Nations—with the result that Kashmir is still today divided and its Pakistan-occupied part a continual source of terrorism flowing into India, as part of the preparation for what Pakistani leaders have called "the need for a second partition of India."

History very seldom records the things that were decisive but took place behind the veil; it records the show in front of the curtain.... My action in giving the movement in Bengal [at the beginning of the century] its militant turn or founding the revolutionary movement is very little known.[135]

*

In some quarters there is the idea that Sri Aurobindo's political standpoint was entirely pacifist, that he was opposed in principle and in practice to all violence and that he denounced terrorism, insurrection, etc., as entirely forbidden by the spirit and letter of the Hindu religion. It is even suggested that he was a forerunner of the gospel of Ahimsa. This is quite incorrect. Sri Aurobindo is neither an impotent moralist nor a weak pacifist.

The rule of confining political action to passive resistance was adopted as the best policy for the National Movement at that stage [in 1905 and after] and not as a part of a gospel of Non-violence or pacifist idealism. Peace is a part of the highest ideal, but it must be spiritual or at the very least psychological in its basis; without a change in human nature it cannot come with any finality. If it is attempted on any other basis (moral principle or gospel of Ahimsa or any other), it will fail and even may leave things worse than before.

...

Sri Aurobindo's position and practice in this matter was the same as Tilak's and that of other Nationalist leaders who were by no means Pacifists or worshippers of Ahimsa.[136]

* *
*

**July 18, 1948**

*(From a letter.)*

I am afraid I can hold out but cold comfort—for the present at least—to those of your correspondents who are lamenting the present state of things. Things are bad, are growing worse and may at any time grow worst or worse than worst if that is possible—and anything however paradoxical seems possible in the present perturbed world. The best thing for them is to realise that all this was necessary because certain possibilities had to emerge and be got rid of, if a new and better world was at all to come into being; it would not have done to postpone them for a later time.... Also they can remember the adage that night is darkest before dawn and that the coming of dawn is inevitable. But they must remember too that the new world whose coming we envisage is not to be made of the same texture as the old and different only in pattern, and that it must come by other means—from within and not from without; so the best way is not to be too much preoccupied with the lamentable things that are happening outside, but themselves to grow within so that they may be ready for the new world, whatever form it may take.[137]

\*\*

**December, 1948**

*(Extracts from a message to the Andhra University,*
*which on December 11 conferred on Sri Aurobindo*
*the Sir Cattamanchi Ramalinga Reddy*
*National Prize.)*

India, shut into a separate existence by the Himalayas and the ocean, has always been the home of a peculiar people with characteristics of its own recognisably distinct from all others, with its own distinct civilisation, way of life, way of the spirit, a separate culture, arts, building of society. It has absorbed all that has entered into it, put upon all the Indian stamp, welded the most diverse elements into its fundamental unity. But it has also been throughout a congeries of diverse peoples, lands, kingdoms and, in earlier times, republics also, diverse races, sub-nations with a marked character of their own, developing different brands or forms of civilisation and culture, many schools of art and architecture which yet succeeded in fitting into the general Indian type of civilisation and culture. India's history throughout has been marked by a tendency, a constant effort to unite all this diversity of elements into a single political whole under a central imperial rule so that India might be politically as well as culturally one. Even after a rift had been created by the irruption of the Mohammedan peoples with their very different religion and social structure, there continued a constant effort of political unification and there was a tendency towards a mingling of cultures and their mutual influence on each other; even some heroic attempts were made to discover or create a common religion built out of these two apparently irreconcilable faiths and here too there were mutual influences.

...

The ancient diversities of the country carried in them great advantages as well as drawbacks. By these differences the country was made the home of many living and pulsating centres of life, art, culture, a richly and brilliantly coloured diversity in unity; all was not drawn up into a few provincial capitals or an imperial metropolis, other towns and regions remaining subordinated and indistinctive or even culturally asleep; the whole nation lived with a full life in its many parts and this increased enormously the creative energy of the whole. There is no possibility any longer that this diversity will endanger or diminish the unity of India. Those vast spaces which kept her people from closeness and a full interplay have been abolished in their separating effect by the march of Science and the swiftness of the means of communication. The idea of federation and a complete machinery for its perfect working have been discovered and will be at full work. Above all, the spirit of patriotic unity has been too firmly established in the people to be easily effaced or diminished, and it would be more endangered by refusing to allow the natural play of life of the sub-nations than by satisfying their legitimate aspirations. The Congress itself in the days before liberation came had pledged itself to the formation of linguistic provinces, and to follow it out, if not immediately, yet as early as may conveniently be, might well be considered the wisest course.* India's national life will then be founded on her natural strengths and the principle of unity in diversity which has always been normal to her and its fulfilment the fundamental course of her being and its very nature, the Many in the One, would place her on the sure foundation of her Swabhava and Swadharma....

A union of States and regional peoples would again be the form of a united India.

...

In this hour, in the second year of its liberation the nation has to awaken to many more very considerable problems, to vast possibilities opening before her but also to dangers and difficulties that may, if not wisely dealt with, become formidable.... There are deeper issues for India herself, since by following certain tempting directions she may conceivably become a nation like many others evolving an opulent industry and commerce, a powerful organisation of social and

---

* The formation of Indian states along linguistic lines in the following years, while meeting Sri Aurobindo's suggestion on the surface, was in practice accompanied by such a high degree of centralization and all-pervasive bureaucratization that the "natural play of life" of the provinces was stifled rather than encouraged; the rigid and uniform machinery of parliamentary representation imposed on the states, which admittedly has served mainly to generate corruption and foster divisions, was also hardly capable of providing the "perfect working" Sri Aurobindo had in mind for an Indian federation.

political life, an immense military strength, practising power-politics with a high degree of success, guarding and extending zealously her gains and her interests, dominating even a large part of the world, but in this apparently magnificent progression forfeiting its Swadharma, losing its soul. Then ancient India and her spirit might disappear altogether and we would have only one more nation like the others and that would be a real gain neither to the world nor to us. There is a question whether she may prosper more harmlessly in the outward life yet lose altogether her richly massed and firmly held spiritual experience and knowledge. It would be a tragic irony of fate if India were to throw away her spiritual heritage at the very moment when in the rest of the world there is more and more a turning towards her for spiritual help and a saving Light. This must not and will surely not happen; but it cannot be said that the danger is not there. There are indeed other numerous and difficult problems that face this country or will very soon face it. No doubt we will win through, but we must not disguise from ourselves the fact that after these long years of subjection and its cramping and impairing effects a great inner as well as outer liberation and change, a vast inner and outer progress is needed if we are to fulfil India's true destiny.[138]

*
* *

**April, 1950**

*(From a Postcript Chapter to*
The Ideal of Human Unity.*)*

The indwelling deity who presides over the destiny of the race has raised in man's mind and heart the idea, the hope of a new order which will replace the old unsatisfactory order, and substitute for it conditions of the world's life which will in the end have a reasonable chance of establishing permanent peace and well-being.... It is for the men of our day and, at the most, of tomorrow to give the answer. For, too long a postponement or too continued a failure will open the way to a series of increasing catastrophes which might create a too prolonged and disastrous confusion and chaos and render a solution too difficult or impossible; it might even end in something like an irremediable crash not only of the present world-civilisation but of all civilisation.

. . .

The terror of destruction and even of large-scale extermination created by these ominous discoveries\* may bring about a will in the governments and peoples to ban and prevent the military use of these inventions, but, so long as the nature of mankind has not changed, this prevention must remain uncertain and precarious and an unscrupulous ambition may even get by it a chance of secrecy and surprise and the utilisation of a decisive moment which might conceivably give it victory and it might risk the tremendous chance.[139]

\*

*(In October, 1950, six months after Sri Aurobindo*
*wrote what follows, China invaded Tibet; an appeal by*
*Tibet to the United Nations fell on deaf ears, and India*

---

\* A reference to the recent discovery and use of nuclear weapons.

*remained a silent spectator. In October, 1962, China
launched an offensive on India's northern borders.)*

In Asia a more perilous situation has arisen, standing sharply
across the way to any possibility of a continental unity of the
peoples of this part of the world, in the emergence of Communist China. This creates a gigantic bloc which could easily
englobe the whole of Northern Asia in a combination between
two enormous Communist Powers, Russia and China, and
would overshadow with a threat of absorption South-Western
Asia and Tibet and might be pushed to overrun all up to the
whole frontier of India, menacing her security and that of
Western Asia with the possibility of an invasion and an
overrunning and subjection by penetration or even by over-
whelming military force to an unwanted ideology, political
and social institutions and dominance of this militant mass
of Communism whose push might easily prove irresistible.
In any case, the continent would be divided between two
huge blocs which might enter into active mutual opposition
and the possibility of a stupendous world-conflict would
arise dwarfing anything previously experienced....[140]

*
* *

**April 4, 1950**

*(From a letter to a disciple.)*

You have expressed in one of your letters your sense of the
present darkness in the world round us.... For myself, the
dark conditions do not discourage me or convince me of the
vanity of my will to "help the world", for I knew they had to
come; they were there in the world nature and had to rise up
so that they might be exhausted or expelled and a better world
freed from them might be there. After all, something has been
done in the outer field and that may help or prepare for getting
something done in the inner field also. For instance, India is

free and her freedom was necessary if the Divine Work was to be done. The difficulties that surround her now and may increase for a time, especially with regard to the Pakistan imbroglio, were also things that had to come and to be cleared out. Nehru's efforts to prevent the inevitable clash are not likely to succeed for more than a short time and so it is not necessary to give him the slap you wanted to go to Delhi to administer to him. Here too there is sure to be a full clearance, though unfortunately, a considerable amount of human suffering in the process is inevitable. Afterwards the work for the Divine will become more possible and it may well be that the dream, if it is a dream, of leading the world towards the spiritual Light, may even become a reality. So I am not disposed even now, in these dark conditions, to consider my will to help the world as condemned to failure.[141]

*
\* \*

**June 28, 1950**

*(From a letter.)*

I do not know why you want a line of thought to be indicated to you for your guidance in the affair of Korea.\* There is nothing to hesitate about there, the whole affair is as plain as a pike-staff. It is the first move in the Communist plan of campaign to dominate and take possession first of these northern parts and then of South East Asia as a preliminary to their manoeuvres with regard to the rest of the continent—in passing, Tibet as a gate opening to India.\* \* If they succeed, there is no reason why domination of the whole world should not follow by steps....[142]

*
\* \*

---

\* A few days earlier, North Korean forces launched an attack on South Korea with Soviet support; Chinese troops joined in a few months later.
\*\* China invaded Tibet four months later, in October.

*(Some forty years earlier, on September 18, 1909,
Sri Aurobindo wrote ... )*

The end of a stage of evolution is usually marked by a powerful recrudescence of all that has to go out of the evolution.

\*
\* \*

**November, 1950**

*(From Sri Aurobindo's last writings.)*

This world is not really created by a blind force of Nature: even in the Inconscient the presence of the supreme Truth is at work; there is a seeing Power behind it which acts infallibly and the steps of the Ignorance itself are guided even when they seem to stumble.... In this vast and apparently confused mass of existence there is a law, a one truth of being, a guiding and fulfilling purpose of the world-existence.[143]

\*
\* \*

*On December 5, 1950, Sri Aurobindo left his body. For ten years he had worked to free India from the clutches of an alien rule; for forty years thereafter he laboured to free the earth from the clutches of a dying age. But among all the nations of the world, India always held a special place in his consciousness: to him she was the Mother, a being with a unique mission and destiny in these birth throes of a new age.*

*For a long time now, the ancient Mother has lain prostrate, half slumbering, half decaying, a prey to a thousand cancers. But even today, if we awaken to what makes her a country unlike any other, if we rediscover in ourselves the simple secret of her ancient Shakti, if we see her bleeding flesh and hear her prayer to us, we can yet bring about her rebirth.*

*<br>* *

**June 6, 1967**

*(An inner communication from<br>Sri Aurobindo to Mother.)*

All the countries live in falsehood.
If only one country stood courageously for truth,
the world might be saved.[144]

# Chronology

| | |
|---|---|
| 1872, Aug. 15 | - Sri Aurobindo is born in Calcutta; he spends his first years at Rangpur (now in Bangladesh), and at the age of 5 is sent to Loreto Convent School, Darjeeling. |
| 1878, Feb. 21 | - Mother is born in Paris. |
| 1879, June | - Sri Aurobindo leaves India for England with his parents and his two elder brothers. He spends 5 years in Manchester, enters St. Paul's School, London, in 1884, and King's College, Cambridge, in 1890. |
| 1885, Dec. | - First session of the Indian National Congress at Bombay. |
| 1886, Aug. 16 | - Sri Ramakrishna passes away. |
| 1892, August | - Sri Aurobindo passes the I.C.S.; he does not appear at a riding test and is disqualified. |
| 1893, Feb. 6 | - Lands at Bombay and soon joins the State service of the Maharaja Gaekwad of Baroda. From August 1893 to March 1894, contributes a series of articles, "New Lamps for Old," to the *Indu Prakash*. |
| 1893, May 31 | - Swami Vivekananda sails for America. |
| 1894, April 8 | - Bankim Chandra Chatterji passes away. In July-August, Sri Aurobindo writes a series of articles on him in the *Indu Prakash*. |
| 1897 | - Sri Aurobindo teaches French, then English at the Baroda College; he will become its Vice-Principal in 1905. |
| 1897, Jan. 15 | - Swami Vivekananda lands at Colombo, and on his way north delivers many lectures throughout India. |
| c. 1900 | - Sri Aurobindo makes first contacts with secret societies in Maharashtra and Bengal. |
| 1901, April 30 | - Sri Aurobindo marries Mrinalini Bose. |
| 1902, July 4 | - Swami Vivekananda passes away. |
| 1905 | - Sri Aurobindo writes *Bhawani Mandir*, a revolutionary pamphlet. |
| | - Partition of Bengal, beginning of the Swadeshi movement. |
| 1906, June | - Sri Aurobindo leaves Baroda for good. |

| | |
|---|---|
| 1906, August | - Bepin Chandra Pal launches the *Bande Mataram* (English daily); Sri Aurobindo joins it and soon becomes its editor.<br>- On August 15, the Bengal National College opens with Sri Aurobindo as its principal. |
| 1906, Dec. | - At its Calcutta session presided over by Dadabhai Naoroji, the Congress declares Swaraj to be its goal. |
| 1907, Aug. 16 | - Sri Aurobindo is arrested for the publication of seditious writings in the *Bande Mataram*; released on bail. He resigns his post of principal of the Bengal National College, giving on August 23 a speech to the students and teachers. Acquitted a month later. |
| 1907, Dec. | - At the Surat session of the Congress, the Nationalist party with Sri Aurobindo presiding over its conference breaks away from the Moderates.<br>- First session of the Muslim League at Karachi. |
| 1908, January | - In Baroda, Sri Aurobindo meets Vishnu Bhaskar Lele, a Maharashtrian yogi, and experiences the Brahman consciousness. Gives many speeches on his way back to Calcutta. |
| 1907-1908 | - Many Nationalist leaders, such as Lala Lajpat Rai, Tilak, Ashwini Kumar Dutt, etc., are deported under various repressive laws. The Nationalist movement goes underground. |
| 1908, May 2 | - Sri Aurobindo is arrested in the Alipore Bomb Case; spends a year in jail and is acquitted on May 6, 1909. |
| 1909 | - The Morley-Minto reforms provide separate electorates for Indian Muslims. |
| 1909, May 30 | - Sri Aurobindo's famous Uttarpara speech. |
| 1909, June 19 | - First issue of the *Karmayogin* (English weekly). |
| 1909, Aug. 23 | - First issue of the *Dharma* (Bengali weekly). |
| 1910, February | - Sri Aurobindo abruptly leaves Calcutta for Chandernagore; on March 31, he will leave for Pondicherry. |
| 1910, April 4 | - Sri Aurobindo reaches Pondicherry.<br>- Charged with sedition for an article in the *Karmayogin* (the charge will be rejected in November). |

| 1914, March 29 | - First meeting with Mother. |
|---|---|
| 1914, June | - Tilak is released from a six-year-long deportation to Burma. |
| 1914, Aug. 15 | - First issue of the *Arya* (English monthly), which will appear until January, 1921. |
| 1916, Dec. | - "Lucknow Pact" between the Congress and the Muslim League. |
| 1919-1920 | - Beginning of the Khilafat and non-cooperation movements under the growing leadership of Mahatma Gandhi. |
| 1920 | - Sri Aurobindo turns down several offers to return to British India and to active politics. |
| 1920, April 24 | - Mother returns to Pondicherry from Japan. |
| 1920, Aug. 1 | - Lokmanya Tilak passes away. |
| 1920, October | - Dr. B. S. Munje pays a visit to Sri Aurobindo. |
| 1920, Dec. | - Nagpur session of the Congress; the goal of Swaraj is eclipsed by the Khilafat agitation. |
| 1923, June 5 | - Chittaranjan Das meets Sri Aurobindo. |
| 1923, Sept. | - Creation of the Swarajya Party. |
| 1925, Jan. 5 | - Lala Lajpat Rai and Purushottamdas Tandon meet Sri Aurobindo. |
| 1925, June 16 | - Deshbandu Chittaranjan Das passes away. |
| 1926, Nov. 24 | - Sri Aurobindo withdraws completely to concentrate on his work. |
| 1928, Feb. 16 | - Rabindranath Tagore meets Sri Aurobindo. |
| 1928, Nov. 17 | - Lala Lajpat Rai passes away a few weeks after having been assaulted by the police during a demonstration at Lahore. |
| 1929, Dec. | - The Lahore session of the Congress, presided over by Jawaharlal Nehru, adopts the goal of complete independence. |
| 1930-1932 | - Three Round Table Conferences with, in August 1932, the Communal Award which hardens divisions between Hindus and Muslims. Savage repression of the Civil Disobedience Movement by the British rulers. |
| 1937 | - Formation of Congress ministries in the Provinces. |
| 1938, Nov. 24 | - Sri Aurobindo breaks his leg while walking in concentration. |

| | |
|---|---|
| 1939, Sept. | - World War II breaks out; the Provincial ministries resign in October-November. |
| 1940, March | - The Muslim League, in session at Lahore, formally demands the creation of Pakistan. |
| 1940, Sept. 19 | - Sri Aurobindo's declaration in support of the Allies. |
| 1941, March | - Subhas Bose, having escaped from detention in Calcutta, arrives in Germany. |
| 1941, Aug. 7 | - Rabindranath Tagore passes away. |
| 1942, March 31 | - Sri Aurobindo publicly supports Cripps' proposals; the Congress turns them down. |
| 1942, April | - The Japanese overrun Burma and bomb cities on India's east coast. |
| 1942, Aug. 9 | - Start of the "Quit India" movement; Mahatma Gandhi and other leaders are arrested soon afterwards. |
| 1944, July | - Subhas Bose's Indian National Army and the Japanese are repulsed in Manipur. |
| 1946, Aug. 16 | - The Muslim League launches its "Direct Action" plan; bloody riots follow in Bengal and Bihar. |
| 1946, Sept. 2 | - Formation of the Interim Government, which the Muslim League joins a month later. |
| 1947, March 24 | - Lord Mountbatten is the new Viceroy. |
| 1947, June | - On the 3rd, Mountbatten announces the British government's final decision to grant India independence on the basis of partition; on the 14th, the Congress accepts the partition of India and the creation of Pakistan. |
| 1947, Aug. 15 | - India's Independence; Sri Aurobindo's 75th birthday. |
| 1947, October | - Pakistan attacks Kashmir; the Indian army repels Pakistani troops, but Nehru calls a halt to the fighting and takes the dispute to the United Nations. |
| 1948, Jan. 30 | - Mahatma Gandhi is assassinated. |
| 1950, October | - China invades Tibet; India remains a silent spectator. |
| 1950, Dec. 5 | - Sri Aurobindo leaves his body. Mother continues his work. |

# References

We give below, section by section, either detailed references or, when these would be too cumbersome to list in full, guides to the sources. The bold numerals refer to the volumes of the Centenary Edition of Sri Aurobindo's works (Sri Aurobindo Ashram, Pondicherry, 1972); they are followed by the page number. "A. & R." refers to the *Archives and Research* half-yearly series published from Pondicherry.

The reader wishing to know more about Sri Aurobindo's immense contribution to India is invited to study the following titles: *Bande Mataram, The Karmayogin, The Secret of the Veda, Essays on the Gita, The Foundations of Indian Culture, On Himself*, as well as Sri Aurobindo's talks with disciples: *Evening Talks* (noted by A. B. Purani) and *Talks with Sri Aurobindo* (four volumes noted by Nirodbaran).

For a general introduction to Sri Aurobindo's life, thought and work, we recommend Satprem's *Sri Aurobindo or the Adventure of Consciousness* (Institut de Recherches Évolutives, Paris, & Mira Aditi, Mysore, 1996).

# I

Nearly all the texts in this section are from the *Bande Mataram* for the years 1893 to 1908 (vol. 1 in Cent. Ed., also with articles in vol. 17 and vol. 27), and from the *Karmayogin* for the years 1909-1910 (vol. 2, also with articles in vol. 3 and 17). Exceptions are:

1. **3**.125-127
2. **3**.181
3. *The Life of Sri Aurobindo* by A. B. Purani (1978), p. 82
4. *On Himself*, **26**.29-32
5. A. & R., April 1978, p. 13-18
6. A. & R., April 1979, p. 4
7. A. & R., December 1978, p. 111
8. A. & R., April 1979, p. 1-4
9. *Sri Aurobindo in the First Decade of the Century* by Manoj Das, p. 137
10. Ibid., p. 134
11. *On Himself*, **26**.34
12. A. & R., April 1977, p. 56-58
13. **3**.454-456
14. **3**.460
15. A. & R., December 1979, p. 196-199
16. Ibid., p. 200-201

# II

Excerpts from letters to Motilal Roy are found in vol. 27 (p. 463 to 499). Other references are:

17. *On Himself,* **26**.27, 37-38
18. A. & R., April 1981, p. 1-6
19. A. & R., April 1983, p. 47
20. A. & R., December 1980, p. 187-194
21. Ibid., p. 194
22. A. & R., December 1977, p. 84
23. A. & R., April 1983, p. 21
24. **3**.116-117
25. **27**.182-183
26. A. & R., December 1983, p. 100, 124
27. A. & R., December 1984, p. 132, 136
28. A. & R., December 1985, p. 152, 168
29. A. & R., April 1979, p. 93-94
30. Ibid., p. 94
31. See *The Politics of History,* by Navaratna S. Rajaram (Voice of India, 1995)
32. *Thoughts and Aphorisms* (in vol. **17**)
33. *The Secret of the Veda,* **10**.3
34. **17**.393-394
35. *The Secret of the Veda,* **10**.33-37
36. *Sri Aurobindo—His Life Unique,* by Rishabhchand, p. 410-411
37. **16**.402-403
38. **17**.335
39. *On Himself,* **26**.424
40. Ibid., **26**.425
41. *The Secret of the Veda,* **10**.352-353
42. **16**.311
43. **17**.277-279
44. **17**.337-341
45. **17**.299
46. **16**.317-319
47. *Thoughts and Glimpses,* **16**.391
48. *The Ideal of Human Unity,* **15**.340
49. *The Human Cycle,* **15**.3-8
50. *The Secret of the Veda,* **10**.439
51. *Hymns to the Mystic Fire,* **11**.9-18
52. *Essays on the Gita,* **13**.37-42
53. Ibid., **13**.44-45
54. Ibid., **13**.52-54
55. *The Human Cycle,* **15**.69-73
56. **16**.392-394
57. *The Ideal of Human Unity,* **15**.492-493
58. *The Hour of God* (1991), p. 3-4
59. A. & R., December 1984, p. 190
60. **17**.351, 357
61. **27**.505-507
62. *The Human Cycle,* **15**.209-213
63. Ibid., **15**.230
64. Ibid., **15**.243
65. Ibid., **15**.250-252
66. *The Renaissance in India,* **14**.401-404
67. *War and Self-Determination,* **15**.598
68. Ibid., **15**.605-606
69. *The Renaissance in India,* **14**.426-433
70. *The Foundations of Indian Culture,* **14**.1-11
71. *War and Self-Determination,* **15**.588-597
72. *The Foundations of Indian Culture,* **14**.27, 31
73. Ibid., **14**.73-75
74. Ibid., **14**.90
75. *Essays on the Gita,* **13**.367-372
76. *The Foundations of Indian Culture,* **14**.122-130
77. **17**.179
78. *War and Self-Determination,* **15**.635
79. *On Himself,* **26**.430-431
80. Original Bengali text in A. & R., April 1980, p.1-10
81. **16**.331
82. **2**.431
83. *On Himself,* **26**.432-433
84. **17**.194-196
85. *The Foundations of Indian Culture,* **14**.363-381
86. *On Himself,* **26**.437
87. Ibid., **26**.438-439

# III

Most of the excerpts from Sri Aurobindo's talks in this section are from A. B. Purani's *Evening Talks*. Others are from talks noted by Anilbaran (published in *Sri Aurobindo Circle*), and from unpublished notations by Pavitra.

88. *History of the Freedom Movement
in India,* by R. C. Majumdar
(Firma KLM, 1988), Vol. III, p. 81

# IV

89. **17.**7-8
90. *On Himself,* **26.**126
91. Ibid., **26.**483
92. Ibid., **26.**122, 124
93. *The History of the Freedom
Movement in India,* Vol. III, p. 310
94. *On Himself,* **26.**468-469
95. Unpublished portion of a letter to
Dilip Kumar Roy
96. Ibid., **26.**165
97. *Letters on Yoga,* **22.**178
98. Ibid., **22.**152
99. *The Liberator* by Sisirkumar Mitra
(Jaico, 1970), p. 199
100. *On Himself,* **26.**375-376
101. *Letters on Yoga,* **22.**196-198
102. Ibid., **24.**1608-1609
103. Ibid., **23.**716
104. Ibid., **23.**717

105. *On Himself,* **26.**167
106. **22.**208-209
107. Ibid., **26.**143
108. *Letters on Yoga,* **22.**205
109. *On Himself,* **26.**125
110. Ibid., **22.**153
111. Ibid., **22.**490
112. Ibid., **22.**144 (2nd paragraph only)
113. *On Himself,* **26.**389
114. Ibid., **26.**135
115. *Letters on Yoga,* **22.**490
116. *Letters on Yoga,* **22.**140
117. *On Himself,* **26.**380
118. *Letters on Yoga,* **23.**665-666
119. Ibid., **22.**139
120. Ibid., **22.**486-487
121. *Correspondence with Sri
Aurobindo* by Nirodbaran, 2.1185

# V

All passages in this section are from *Evening Talks* (noted by A. B. Purani)
and *Talks with Sri Aurobindo* (noted by Nirodbaran).

# VI

122. *The Life Divine,* **19.**1053-1056
123. *On Himself,* **26.**394
124. Ibid.
125. Ibid., **26.**399
126. Ibid., **26.**396-398
127. Ibid., **26.**129-130
128. Ibid., **26.**167-168
129. Ibid., **26.**168-169
130. *Letters on Yoga,* **22.**424-425
131. *Champaklal Speaks* (1976), p. 66
132. *On Himself,* **26.**169-170
133. Ibid., **26.**401-402
134. Ibid., **26.**46

135. Ibid., **26.**49
136. Ibid., **26.**22
137. Ibid., **26.**171-172
138. Ibid., **26.**407-413
139. *The Ideal of Human Unity,*
**15.**563-565
140. Ibid., **15.**567
141. Partially in *On Himself,* **26.**172
142. Ibid., **26.**416
143. *The Supramental Manifestation
upon Earth,* **16.**73
144. *Mother's Agenda* Vol. 8, p. 173

# Index

## A

Adya Shakti, 21
Afghanistan, 170, 229
Agni, 116-117
agriculture, 39
  see also peasantry, village
Ahimsa, 55, 123, 151, 168, 218-219, 246
  see also non-violence
Ajatashatru, 96
Alipore Bomb Case, 46*(fn)*, 150, 159
Alipore jail, 47, 48, 214
Allies (in World War II), 226, 236, 238-239
altruism, 80, 102, 112
Ambedkar, B. R., 204-205
America, 59, 81, 174, 237
Americans, 77, 239
Andhra University, 247
Anusilan Samiti, 13
Arabians, 190
archaeology, 98*(fn)*, 100-101*(fn)*
Arjuna, 51, 125, 206, 240
art, 65-68, 103, 127, 182, 220
  Indian art, 59-60, 67, 68, 168
Arya (English monthly), 83, 111
Arya Samaj, 170
Aryan, 49, 106
  character and life, 52, 60
  fighter, 126
  invasion (theory of), 96, 98, 100-101*(fn)*, 107-108, 114, 115, 116
  language, 97-98, 108-109
  people, 106-107, 108, 153
  worker, 113
asceticism, 92, 106-107, 112, 142-143, 149, 198, 240
Asia, 25, 39, 157, 178
  and the Communist plan, 252-253
astronomy, 168
Augustus, 77
avatar, 49, 89, 91, 102
Azad, Abul Kalam, Maulana, 230, 238*(fn)*

## B

Bahaism, 169

Baker, Edward, 47*(fn)*
Bakunin, 93
Bande Mataram (mantra and national song), 9, 21-22, 37, 154, 222-223
Bande Mataram (English daily), 17, 27, 47
Banerjee, Jatindranath, 13
Banerji, Surendranath, 17
Bangladesh, 15*(fn)*
Bankim, see under Chatterji
Baptista, Joseph, 148
barbarians, 126
barbarism, 103, 127, 175, 239
Barin, see under Ghose
Baroda, 11, 35
Baroda College, 11
battle, 45-46, 51, 102, 123-126, 143-144, 206-207, 238-240
beauty, 66, 68, 103, 127, 217-218, 220
Bengal, 39, 111-112, 152, 153, 222, 246
  atrocities on Hindus in, 203, 241-242
  awakening of, 21-22, 67*(fn)*, 180
  partition of, 17, 18, 54*(fn)*
Bengal National College, 27
Bhagavat Gita, 46, 48, 52, 125-126, 170, 171, 176, 183, 201, 206
Bharati, Subramania, 109*(fn)*
Bhawani Mandir, 13
Bible, 68, 170, 176, 190
birth control, 185-186
  see also overpopulation
Bolshevism, 151, 183, 200, 203
Bose, Subhas Chandra, 223, 230, 231, 237*(fn)*
Brahmanas, 95, 105
brahmateja, 50
Brahmins, 28-29, 44, 55, 87, 120-121, 208
Britain, see under England
British, the, see under English
British rule (in India), 9, 18-19, 31, 40*(fn)*, 43, 46*(fn)*, 60-61, 158, 178, 202, 219*(fn)*, 230, 231
Buddha, 92, 106, 144, 204, 213
Buddhism, 92, 112, 129, 137, 177
bureaucracy, 58, 68, 135, 220
business, 216, 240

263

# C

Caliph (Sultan of Turkey), 149*(fn)*
capitalism, 154, 200
capitalists, 77, 103, 221
caste, 44, 79, 90, 207-208
  original meaning of, 28-30, 120, 177
  perversion of, 119, 120-121
  political use of, 18, 32, 192*(fn)*
*caturvarna/cāturvarnya*, 90, 120
Chaitanya, 204
Chandala, 29, 44
Chandernagore, 71
Chandragupta Maurya, 178
charity, 102, 112, 129
  *see also* altruism
Charkha, 170, 215, 219, 225
Charlemagne, 77
Chatterji, Bankim Chandra, 9, 21, 155
China, 88, 137, 202, 220
  Communist China, 252
  and India, 252, 253
  and Tibet, 252, 253
Chokha Mela, 29
Christ, 77, 137, 142, 144, 170, 175, 205, 213
Christianity, 59, 129, 142-143, 170, 175-176, 184, 217
Christians, 63, 68, 171, 183
civilization, 96, 99, 100, 126-227, 142
  ancient, 96, 100, 117
  present, 127, 134, 235, 236, 241, 251
  *see also* Indian, Western civilization
commercialism, 61, 67, 127, 140, 153, 216
Communism, 90, 103, 154, 174, 214, 220-221, 252, 253
Communists (Indian), 231
Confucians, 190
Congress, *see under* Indian National Congress
Congressmen, 222
conversion, 204-205
  of Hindus into Muslims, 167, 245
Coomaraswamy, A. K., 60*(fn)*
corruption, 209, 222
courage, 22-23, 25, 30, 36, 54, 57, 58, 68, 124, 148, 154
Cowell, E. B., 97*(fn)*
creation (new), 21, 23, 32, 57, 91, 128, 154, 193, 200-201, 241, 244, 247

criminals,
  Indian, 214
  in politics, 221
Cripps, Sir Stafford, 237
Cripps' proposal, 224*(fn)*, 237
culture, *see under* Indian culture
Curzon, 17
Czechoslovakia, 231

# D

Danton, 24
Das, Chittaranjan, 13, 47, 159, 185, 216, 221, 223, 242
Dayananda Saraswati, 116-118, 170
democracy, 61, 62, 103-104, 149, 174, 214
  Indian conception of, 39
  parliamentary, 93, 172, 214, 221
  in the West, 103
  *see also* political systems
destruction, 21, 91, 123-124, 128, 241
  means of, 228, 251
Deuskar, Sakharam Ganesh, 40*(fn)*
Devil, 143
*Dharma* (Bengali weekly), 47
*dharma*, 48*(fn)*, 69-70, 151, 152, 182
  in ancient times, 165, 177
  basis of democracy, 39
  India's, 49, 158
  *see also sanātana dharma*
dictatorship, 214
diplomacy, 37, 45
divide-and-rule, 17, 18-19, 230
Dominion status (for India), 223-224, 231, 237
Dravidian
  languages, 97, 98*(fn)*, 108-109
  races, 49*(fn)*, 96, 98, 107-109, 114, 115, 116
  *see also* Aryan invasion
Duraiswamy Iyer, 237*(fn)*
Durga, 124, 222-223
Dutt, Ashwini Kumar, 17
Dutt, Romesh, 40*(fn)*
Dwaraka, 100-101*(fn)*

# E

East, 25, 88
economy, 43, 156, 200, 220, 221

Western system of, 42, 127
India's ruined by Britain, 40*(fn)*, 43, 202
education, 11-12, 127, 216, 220
  artistic, 66-67,
  British/European, 39, 43, 52, 55, 59, 60, 65, 183, 220
  language/medium of, 75, 157
  moral or religious, 73
  national, 23, 27, 35, 38, 67, 133, 180
  scientific, 65
  teaching by snippets, 74-76
Egypt (ancient), 137
England, 24, 60-61, 67, 202, 236, 239
English,
  the English, 24, 43, 67, 71, 217, 239
  their coming to India, 60-61, 178
  language, 157
  *see also* British rule, Europe
Europe, 55, 59, 88, 104, 152, 217
  and Asia, 25, 39
  bankruptcy of, 77-82, 114-115, 175, 218
  her religious history, 59, 147
  her Shakti, 152
  *see also* education, materialism, politics, religion, scholarship
Europeanization
  of India, 42, 43, 52, 59-61, 71-72, 86-87, 140, 223
  of Japan, 88, 216, 218
evil, 124, 143, 171, 182
evolution, 51, 59, 65, 136, 189, 201, 217, 235, 254
  the new evolution, 111
  *see also* supermind, truth
Extremism, 32*(fn)*

### F

fanaticism, 147, 167, 169, 190, 197, 204
Fascism, 194, 214, 226
fast, *see under* hunger strike
federation (for India), 249
fight, *see under* battle
force (spiritual), *see under* power
forests, 220
France, 202, 227-228
freedom, 26, 79, 213, 214, 228
French Revolution, 77, 80
Freud, Sigmund, 218

future, 25-26, 57, 60, 65, 72, 74, 76, 92, 94, 99, 101, 110, 112, 118-119, 129, 141, 142, 201, 236, 241, 247

### G

Gandhi, Devadas, 170
Gandhi, M. K., Mahatma, 9, 151, 170, 180, 191-192, 202-203, 206, 226, 230
  and birth control, 186
  and castes, 207-208
  and Charkha, 215-216, 219, 225
  a Christian, 175-176
  and Congress, 209, 215, 219
  and Cripps' proposal, 237-238*(fn)*
  a European, 175
  and hunger-strike, 145, 168, 171
  and Khilafat movement, 173
  and Muslim demands, 227
  and non-cooperation, 160, 180
  and non-violence, 166-168, 218-219, 225, 226
  in South Africa, 105, 168
  and Swaraj, 173*(fn)*
  and World War II, 217, 224, 229-230
Gangoly, O. C., 115-116
Germans, 239
Germany, 112
  in World War II, 213, 236, 237*(fn)*
Ghose, Barindra Kumar, 13, 17, 47, 150
Gita, *see under Bhagavat Gita*
Goethe, 77, 88
Goonda-raj, 203
Goswami, Bijoy, 76
government, 217, 236
  controls, 213
  systems of, 165, 172, 177-178, 214-215
Greece (ancient), 86, 119, 168, 183, 217
Greek (language), 109
Greeks, 158, 179, 183, 213, 217
Griffith, Ralph T. H., 97*(fn)*
*guru*, 119

### H

Haeckel, 87
Harappan cililization, 100*(fn)*
hell, 126, 143, 147

Hindu,
  culture, *see under* Indian culture
  Hindus, 19, 31, 39, 40, 44, 58, 63-65,
  167, 179 190, 201, 222-223, 227,
  241-242, 245
  religion, *see under* Hinduism
  society, *see under* Indian society
Hinduism, 48-50, 55, 69-70, 86-88, 92,
  94, 96, 124, 129, 143, 145-147, 207
  aggressive and expanding, 131
  its central principle, 145-147, 179, 184,
  its decline, 81, 131
  orthodox, 1, 32, 89-90, 94
  passive, 183
  untouched by the Congress, 32
  and violence, 246
  *see also* religion, *sanātana dharma*
Hindu-Muslim question, 17, 18-19, 31,
  53-54, 58, 62-65, 165-166, 167, 173,
  181, 195, 222-223, 227, 228, 230,
  241-242, 244-245
Hitler, 193, 194, 213, 217, 224-226, 227,
  229*(fn)*, 230, 239, 242
  sympathy for, 225
Holland, 226
honesty, 112-113
humanitarianism, 59, 80, 112, 196
humanity, *see under* man/mankind
hunger strike, 145, 168, 171


# I


I.C.S. (Indian Civil Service), 223
idealism, 194, 196, 246
imperialism, 24, 202, 226
India,
  her assimilation of other cultures,
  86, 178-179, 248
  as Bharata Shakti, 139
  as Bhawani Bharati, 15
  her decline/degeneration, 30, 40-41,
  43, 59-60, 61, 85-86, 150-153, 185
  her destiny, 22, 133-134, 139, 245, 250
  her *dharma*/Swadharma, 42, 49, 158,
  165, 177, 250
  her freedom, 149, 160, 209, 219, 226,
  230, 237, 244-245, 252-253
  her future, 61, 72, 92, 94, 110, 112, 149,
  154, 157, 203, 209, 237, 245, 249-250
  her genius/spirit, 61, 149-150, 172, 178
  government for, 172, 178, 215,

220-221, 249
  her greatness, 24, 27-28, 44, 64, 110,
  132, 160
  the guide of the world/*guru* of
  nations, 38, 110
  her Independence, 19, 203, 209, 224
  the laboratory of the soul, 40
  her mission, 1, 92, 112, 139, 140, 154,
  159
  as the Mother, 13, 15, 16, 21-22, 28,
  41, 53, 54, 64, 223, 243, 255
  and the new Truth, 171, 184
  North India, 107-108, 115
  partition of, 17, 224, 244-245
  her past, 30, 38, 55, 60, 61, 64, 98*(fn)*,
  100-101, 137, 157, 165, 172, 177-179,
  184, 195, 201, 204, 214, 217, 247-248
  her rebirth/regeneration, 1, 41, 44,
  57, 88, 92, 93, 110, 140, 153, 154, 158
  her Shakti, 13-15, 152, 157, 158
  South India, 107-108, 115
  her spirituality/spiritual heritage, 24,
  26, 40, 52, 60, 86, 88, 93, 98*(fn)*, 110,
  114-115, 124, 126, 129, 132, 133,
  137-138, 139, 145-146, 154, 158, 175,
  179, 184, 195, 201, 225, 240, 250
  her unity, 62-64, 158, 230, 244-245,
  247-249
  *see also* art, Bengal, British rule,
  education, Hindu, Hinduism, Indian,
  scholarship, etc.
Indian,
  civilization, 24, 30, 64, 81, 85, 98*(fn)*,
  100-101*(fn)*, 137, 142, 152, 247-248
  culture, 64, 65, 67, 86, 115, 137, 139,
  140, 145-146, 157, 158, 168, 171, 179,
  222-223, 242, 248
  Indians, 13-15, 52, 60, 139, 146,
  150-153, 175, 185, 213-214
  intellect/mind, 12, 43, 87-88, 95,
  111-112, 126, 147, 157
  mentality, 225, 228
  society, 85-86, 89-90, 92, 119-121,
  131, 165
  universities, 11, 12, 60
Indian National Congress, 9, 17, 19, 43,
  132, 149, 155-156, 219, 241*(fn)*, 249
  and the communal principle, 19, 53,
  195
  corruption in, 209
  a Fascist organization, 215
  imitation of, 61-62

and the Indian people, 18, 32
and Jinnah, 223
its leaders, 10, 20
and Pakistan, 224
and the Partition, 244
sessions of,
-Amritsar (1919), 149
-Calcutta (1906), 35
-Lahore (1929), 149*(fn)*
-Lucknow (1916), 195
-Nagpur (1920), 149*(fn)*, 155
-Surat (1907), 35
and World War II, 227, 231
Indo-Afghan race, 96, 107
Indo-Saracenic architecture, 168
Indra, 116-117
*Indu Prakash* (Bombay daily), 9
Indus-Saraswati civilization, 100*(fn)*
industry, 14, 43, 78, 127, 154, 216, 221
institutions, 9, 71-72, 136, 141, 219
intolerance, 147, 167
Islam, 32, 44, 53, 129, 143, 158, 167, 170,
217, 223
*see also* Muslim
Islamic culture, 168, 179
*itihāsa*, 98*(fn)*

J

Jainism, 151, 176, 177
Jallianwalla Bagh massacre, 156*(fn)*
Japan, 88, 137, 202, 216, 237*(fn)*
Japanese, 216, 218
*jāt*, 90
Jews, 190, 242
Jinnah, 223, 224, 230, 241, 245
Judaism, 129
Judea, 137

K

Kabir, 146
Kāla Purusha, 91
Kali Yuga, 91
Kālī, 44, 106, 124
Kalki, 148
*Karmayogin* (English weekly), 47, 71,
77, 83
Kashmir, 228, 245*(fn)*
Kemal, Mustapha, 169*(fn)*, 192

Khaddar, 170
Khilafat movement, 149*(fn)*, 156*(fn)*,
165, 169, 173, 195
Koran, 170, 190
Korea, 253
Krishna / Vasudeva, 46, 50, 51, 100*(fn)*,
106, 125, 205, 206, 238, 240
Kshatriya, 20, 29, 44, 46, 55, 120-121,
167

L

Lajpat Rai, Lala, 17
language, 75, 129
*see also* Aryan language, Dravidian
languages, Sanskrit
Latin, 109
law, its true function, 45
*see also dharma* and *shastra*
Lenin, 192
literature, 73, 80
love, 14, 91, 153
gospel of, 45-46, 144

M

machinery, 103, 127, 135, 136, 141
exaggerated importance of, 51-52, 71,
79, 81
of the State, 104, 177
*Mahabharata*, 46, 98*(fn)*, 100*(fn)*, 238,
240
Mahomed, 190
Mahomedans, *see under* Muslims
Malaviya, Madan Mohan, Pandit, 166
man/mankind, 44-45, 65, 67, 94, 112,
115, 118, 119, 120, 125, 127, 128, 129,
134, 135, 136, 196, 201, 216, 218
his destiny, 136, 235, 251
in Europe, 78-79
an infant, 193
his intellect, 115, 163, 218
more mental than woman, 181
his nature, 144, 189, 200, 219
a reasoning animal, 85
his status with regard to woman, 90
of today, 213
a transitional being, 189
*see also* civilization, future
Mantra, the future, 37, 155

Manu, 89
Marx, Karl, 200
materialism, 1, 61, 77-78, 80, 85, 92,
  114, 140, 197, 201
mathematics, 168
matter, field of Sri Aurobindo's Yoga,
  189, 193, 194
Maurya, the dynasty, 178
Mayavada, 183
Mazzini, 57, 93
medical science, 102-103
Mesopotamia, 137
Minto, Earl, 47(fn)
  see also Morley-Minto reforms
Mitter, P. (Pramatha Mitra), 13
moderation, moderatism, 89, 93, 118
Mohammedans, see under Muslims
monarchy, 177-178, 214
Monier-Williams, M., 97(fn)
Moonje, B. S., see under Munje
morality, 43, 73, 71, 186, 203, 246
Morley-Minto reforms, 31(fn), 62-63, 64
Moslems, see under Muslims
Mother, 113, 187, 193, 238, 241, 255
the (Great) Mother, 21, 41
  see also India, as the Mother
motherland, see under India, as the
  Mother
Mrinalini Devi, 16
Müller, F. Max, 87, 95, 96-97, 116,
  117(fn)
Mullick, Subodh, 27
Munje, B. S., 155
music, 65, 66
Muslim,
  culture, 168, 179, 222
  League, 31(fn), 195(fn), 224, 241(fn)
  religion, see under Islam
Muslims, 167, 169, 173, 190
  coming to India, 158, 178-179, 248
  Indian Muslims, 31, 44, 53, 58, 169,
  181, 203, 222, 223, 227, 228, 245
  their sense of separateness, 31, 64,
  169(fn)
  see also Hindu-Muslim question
Mussolini, 193, 229(fn)

N

Naoroji, Dadabhai, 35, 40(fn)
Napoleon, 77

Nationalism, 13, 32, 64
  its call, 44
  is sanātana dharma, 50
Nationalist movement/party, 17, 32-33,
  36, 44, 45, 47, 50, 54, 59, 60, 93, 215,
  246
  see also Swadeshi
Nazis/Nazism, 211, 214, 217, 218,
  229(fn), 236
  see also Hitler
Nehru, Jawaharlal, 192(fn), 207,
  228-229, 238(fn), 245(fn), 253
newspapers, see under press
Nivedita, Sister, 13, 71, 219
non-cooperation movement, 156, 160,
  180
non-violence, 45, 151, 166-168, 170,
  218-219, 225, 226, 229, 246
  see also Ahimsa
nuclear weapons, 251

O

obscurantism, 147
occultism, 200
orthodox, see under Hinduism
overpopulation, 63-64
  see also birth control

P

paganism, 129
Pakistan, 15(fn), 224, 227, 241, 245(fn),
253
Pal, Bepin Chandra, 17
Palestine, 137
panchayat (system), 178, 221
Pariah, 29, 208
parliamentary democracy, see
  under democracy
Parsis, 63
partition, see under Bengal, India,
  Pakistan
passive resistance, 93, 151, 167-168,
  219, 246
Patanjali, 111
Patel, Vallabhbhai, Sardar, 243
patriotism, 21-22, 23, 24-25, 76
peace, the gospel of, 45, 125, 246

peasantry, 18, 32, 39, 40, 44
  see also agriculture, village
Persia, 86(fn), 168, 169, 179
Pétain, 227
philanthropy, 112
  see also altruism, charity
poetry, 44, 65, 127, 138
Poland, 231
political systems,
  in ancient India, 137, 165, 172,
    177-178, 214, 220-221, 248,
  in the West, 103-104, 172, 214
  see also Communism, democracy,
    Socialism
politician, 45, 132, 202
  Indian politicians, 173, 182-183,
    184-185, 221, 229
  the qualities of, 20, 25, 202
politics, 18, 20, 41, 45, 55, 149, 240
  European/Western, 149, 151, 153-154
  the field of the Kshatriya, 20
  Indian politics, 93, 110, 151, 153-154,
    171, 177, 182-183, 184
  language of, 31, 138
  spirituality in, 50-51, 57, 61, 93, 132,
    138-139, 149, 184
Pondicherry, 71, 83
population, see under overpopulation
poverty, 40, 102, 112, 220
power (divine, spiritual), 21, 23, 25-26,
    36-37, 55-56, 57, 74, 111, 141, 160,
    184, 236, 238, 254
  see also Shakti, strength
pralaya, 74
press, 80, 174
propaganda, 196
psychoanalysis, 197-198, 218
psychology, 198
Puranas, 69, 96, 100(fn), 105, 110

R

Rajagopalachari, Chakravarti, 166,
    237-238(fn)
Rama, 238
Ramakrishna, 76, 102
Ramakrishna Mission, 112
Ramayana, 98(fn)
Ramdas, 46
Ramprasad, 146
Rao, S. R., 101(fn)

rationalism, 55, 85, 140
reason, 1, 85, 201-202
reforms/reformers, 89-90
religion, 49, 101, 129-130, 169, 182, 190,
    201, 207
  aggressive religions, 183
  degeneration/failure of, 80, 169, 182,
    196
  divorced from life, 51, 68, 139
  European conception of, 50, 68, 139,
    145-146
  Indian conception of, 69, 182
  notion of single religion, 147
  see also Christianity, Hinduism,
    Islam, sanātana dharma, spirituality
renunciation (of life), 106-107, 240
republic (in ancient India), 137, 178, 248
revolution, 37, 38, 110
  era of, 140-141
  spiritual, 129
Rig-Veda, see under Veda
Rishis, 26, 49, 89, 98(fn), 116, 121, 158
Rolland, Romain, 193
Rome (ancient), 80, 119, 137
Roth, Prof. von, 116
Roy, Motilal, 105
Rudra, 123, 144
Russel, Bertrand, 193
Russia, 193, 225, 252
Russians, 176, 217

S

samatā, 206
Samurai, 29, 44
Sanātana dharma, 49-50, 51, 69, 93, 94,
    145
  see also Hinduism
Sannyasin, 69, 106, 219
Sanskrit, 12, 100(fn), 107, 109, 118, 157
Saraswati (river), 101(fn)
Satyagraha, Satyagrahi, 151, 166, 180,
    209
Satya Yuga, 91
Sayana, 94-96, 105, 116
scholarship,
  in Europe, 12, 80, 95-96, 97(fn), 98(fn),
    107, 115, 116
  in India, 12, 98(fn), 115-116
science, 49, 59, 77-78, 80, 110, 127, 134,
    135, 137, 235, 249

in ancient India, 137
in the Veda, 117
its limitation, 197
superstition of, 87, 99
*see also* education
secular (nothing secular), 146, 149
Shakespeare, 77
Shakti, 13-15, 139, 152-153
*see also* India, strength
Shankaracharya, 29, 87, 92, 94-95, 97, 112, 204
Shastra, 69, 86-87, 89, 146
Shiva, 29, 98*(fn)*, 123
Shivaji, 46
Shudras, 29, 119, 120-121
Sikh Gurus, 146
Sikhs, 63
Sinde, Nana Saheb, 218
Socialism/Socialists, 103, 135, 174, 215, 220
soul-force, 124, 191
spiritism, 200
spirituality, 50, 51, 92, 135, 138, 171, 200
age of, 135-136
basis of life, 154, 159, 203, 219
European notion of, 139, 200
of India, *see under* India, her spirituality
in politics, 50-51, 57, 61, 93, 138-139, 149-150, 184
in society, 134, 138-139
spiritualization of life/man, 129, 134-135, 139, 140
Sri Aurobindo's idea of, 149
true spirituality, 139
Sri Aurobindo (main events in his life, chronologically),
return from England, 9
in Baroda service, 11
his revolutionary action, 13, 246
editor of *Bande Mataram*, 17
principal of Bengal National College, 27
behind the Nationalist movement, 195-196, 246
*Bande Mataram* sedition case, 27, 195-196
Surat Congress, 35
Alipore Bomb Case, 47
withdrawal from politics, 71, 110-111, 151
departure for Chandernagore, 71

departure for Pondicherry, 71, 83
meeting with Mother, 113
calls for his return to politics, 148-149, 155-156
his withdrawal in 1926, 187
accident to his leg, 211
his support for the Allies, 231, 236, 238
his public support for Cripps' proposal, 224*(fn)*, 237
his message for India's Independence, 244-245
his passing, 255
*see also Chronology*, p. 257 ff
Srinivas Iyengar, 215
Stalin, 215, 225
strength, 14-15, 16, 18, 21, 32, 36, 45, 52-53, 54, 57, 58, 124, 125-126
*see also* India, Shakti
suffering, 22-23, 166-167, 176, 253
Sufism, 168
supermind, supramental, 173-174, 199, 200
superstition, 55, 85, 87, 90, 95, 99-100, 106, 200
*svadharma*, 177, 182, 250
Swadeshi movement, 17, 35, 39, 40*(fn)*, 156, 180, 183, 195
Swaraj, 17, 35, 56, 93, 180, 209
inner, 53

# T

Tagore, Rabindranath, 17, 27, 193, 194, 215
Tagore, Surendranath, 13
Tamil (language), 109
Tamil saints, 146
Tantra, 105
Taoists, 190
*tapasyā*, 111
taxes, 221
terrorism, 56, 93, 246
theosophy, 94, 200
Tibet, 251-253
Tilak, Bal Gangadhar, Lokmanya, 17, 132, 148, 155, 160, 185, 195, 246
tolerance, 179
Tolstoy/Tolstoyism, 151, 176
tradition, 191, 240-241
tribals, 32, 44

truth, 37, 57, 112, 122, 197
  infinite, 204
  loyalty to, 206-207
  monopoly of, 190
  new Truth, 171, 184, 196, 200-201, 241
  spiritual truth, 202
  supreme Truth, 254
Tukaram, 146
Turkey, 169

# U

unity, 31, 167
  see also Indian
Upanishads, 69, 97, 105, 110, 137, 171,
  194, 201
Uttarpara Speech, 48-49

# V

Vaishyas, 29, 120-121
Vande Mataram, see under Bande
  Mataram
Veda, Vedas, 48, 69, 94-99, 105-109,
  116-118, 170, 190
  date of, 101(fn)
  and India's future, 94
  lost sense of, 95, 96-97, 114
  Rock of the Ages, 97
  scientific knowledge in, 117-118
  secret of, 99, 122
  symbolism of, 98(fn), 114
  viewed by Western scholars, 95-97,
  107, 116-117
Vedanta, 52, 95, 96, 109, 168
Vedic age/civilization, 96, 119-120
Vedic Rishis, see under Rishis
village, 39, 41
  in ancient India, 172, 220
  development, 172, 180
  see also agriculture, peasantry
violence, see under non-violence
virtue, 171
Vishnu, 98(fn), 144
Vivekananda, Swami, 9, 24, 76, 97, 102,
  185, 219
Voltaire, 77

# W

Wakankar, V. S., 101(fn)
war, 81-82, 123-124, 125, 202, 239-240
  see also World War I, II
waste, 198-199, 215
West, 25, 88
  red evening of, 157
  see also Europe
Western civilization, 24(fn), 41, 42, 56,
  59, 77-81, 114, 127-128, 140, 157, 216
Wilson, H. H., 97(fn)
woman, 102, 181, 185
  in ancient India, 119
  in politics, 181
  her status with regard to man, 90
  her subjection, 138
World War I, 124, 125, 216
World War II, 211, 238-239
  Sri Aurobindo's support of the Allies,
  231, 236, 238

# Y - Z

Yajñavalkya, 96
Yaska, 96
Yoga, 48, 52, 69, 109, 137, 159, 186
  national Yoga, 93
  old system of, 150, 194
  Sri Aurobindo's, 144-145, 171, 189,
  191, 193-194, 201, 202, 203
youth, the young, 44, 52, 57, 154
  see also education
Yugantar (Bengali weekly), 17
zamindars, 40(fn)
zenana, 44

Achevé d'imprimer sur les presses de
Thomson Press (Faridabad, Inde) pour
l'Institut de Recherches Évolutives,
janvier 1997

Dépôt légal 1er trimestre 1997